D1097923

The Films of Shirley MacLaine

The Films of Shirley MacLaine

CHRISTOPHER PAUL DENIS

THE CITADEL PRESS SECAUCUS, N.J.

For My Parents,
Paul Denis and Helen Martin Denis

First edition

Published by Citadel Press
A division of Lyle Stuart Inc.
120 Enterprise Ave., Secaucus, N. J. 07094
In Canada: General Publishing Co. Limited
Don Mills, Ontario
Manufactured in the United States of America by
Halliday Lithograph, West Hanover, Mass.
Designed by William R. Meinhardt

Library of Congress Cataloging in Publication Data

Denis, Christopher.
The films of Shirley MacLaine.

1. MacLaine, Shirley, 1934- 2. Moving-picture actors and actresses—United States—Biography.
3. Moving-pictures—Plots, themes, etc. I. Title.
PN2287.M18D4 791.43′028′0924 [B] 80-12171
ISBN 0-8065-0693-8

Acknowledgments

This volume would not have been possible without the invaluable aid of the following individuals and organizations:

Metro-Goldwyn-Mayer Pictures
Paramount Pictures
Seven Arts Productions
20th Century-Fox
United Artists Corporation
Universal Pictures
Warner Bros.
Staff at the Library for the Performing Arts at Lincoln Center
Jerry Ohlinger's Movie Material Store
Movie Star News
Audience Services Department at CBS-TV
Program Analysis Department at NBC-TV
Program Information Department at ABC-TV
Las Vegas Convention Bureau
Gene Andrewski, Joan and Jack Brandon, Philip Castanza, Sally DeMay, Michael Denis, Werner Erhard, Jack L. Green of ICM, Jonas Halpern of Warner Bros., Bill Hayes, Dick Maurice, Judy Samelson, Susan Sharp, Stephanie Shulman of WNET-TV, Dr. Richard Resnick, Dr. Melvin Thrash, Peter Vega, and especially my friend Lyle Stuart, who gave me the chance.
Special acknowledgment: James M. Seward, Co-Trustee of the Estate of Edward R. Murrow.

Contents

I think of myself as a communicator, not an entertainer. I communicate what I'm feeling. What I'm thinking. What I believe. What I don't believe. I communicate what I think is funny. What I think is sad. What I think is loving.

—Shirley MacLaine

Shirley MacLaine's Biography

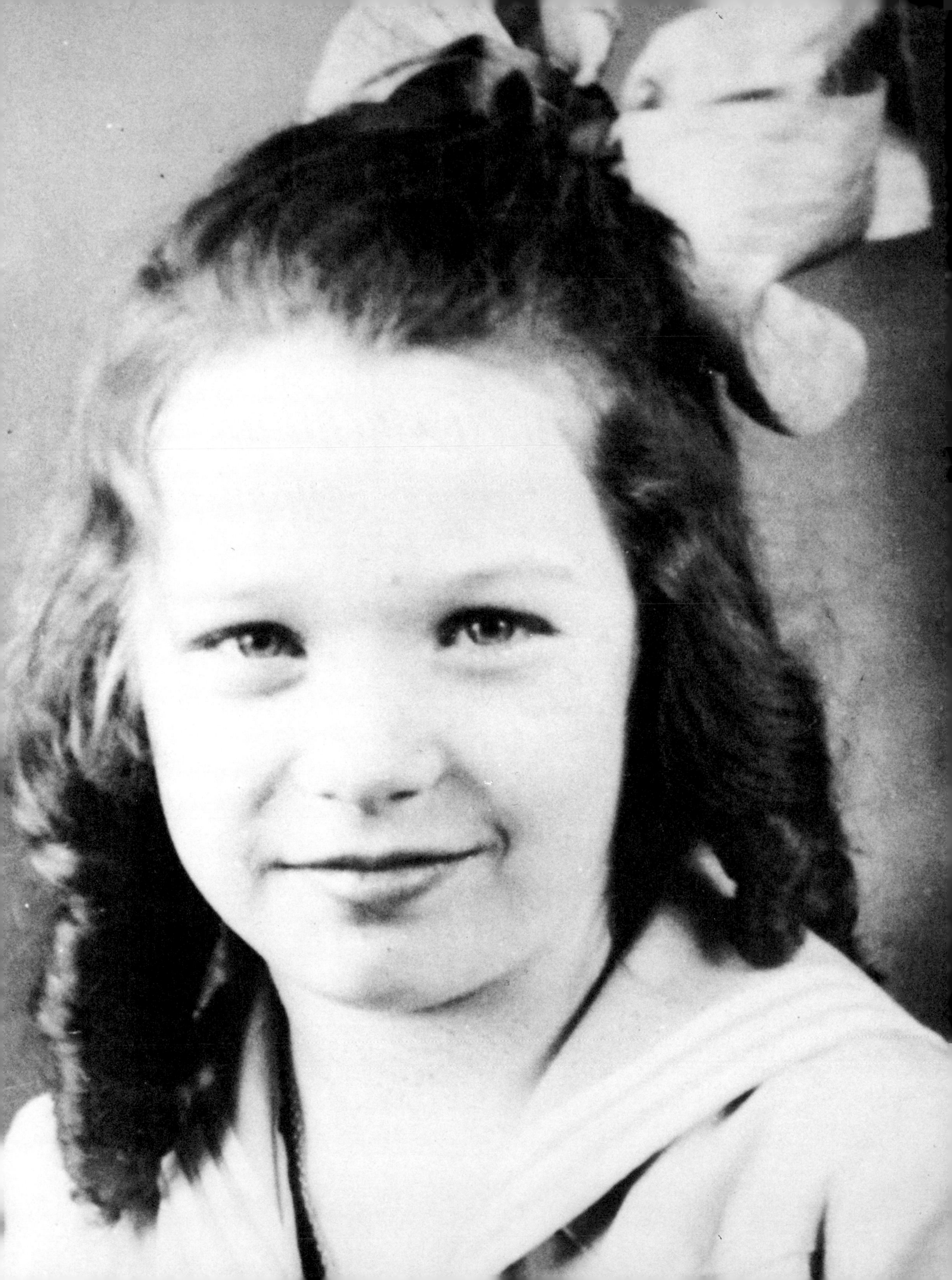

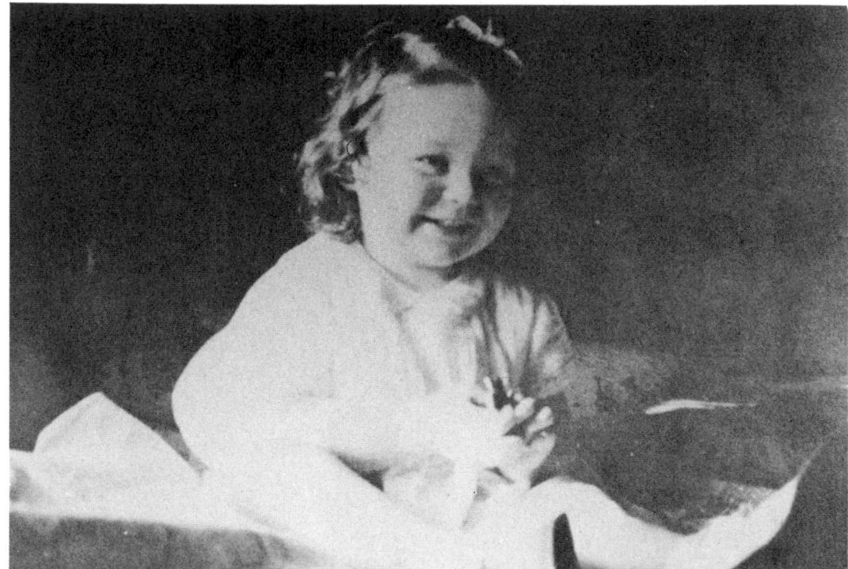

Shirley, not yet out of baby shoes, was a beautiful child.

Warren and Shirley on the lawn in front of their home, about 1940.

Shirley and Warren stand by their father's car in Arlington, Virginia, in the early 1940s.

Shirley MacLaine's performance in *The Turning Point* moved film critic Rex Reed to write, "Shirley MacLaine explodes with honesty and moment-to-moment naturalism. It is her best role in years, and she seizes the role with her teeth like raw steak."

This statement could describe Shirley MacLaine in her personal life, too.

Her life, like an urgent telegram, is one of frenetic activity, but every gesture, every breath has a purpose. She is always working on, or with, something important.

She has starred in thirty films; written, produced, and co-directed a documentary about China; been nominated five times for Academy Awards; written two bestselling autobiographical books; finished her first novel; starred in Broadway shows and nightclubs; headed her own television series; has twice been a delegate to the Democratic National Convention; campaigned with John and Bobby Kennedy and George McGovern; and won three Emmy Awards for her TV specials. In addition, she singly supports orphanages in India and Japan and was chair-

Early on, Shirley displayed a look of self-confidence and determination as well as a sweet wholesomeness.

person of the Tom Dooley Foundation, bringing hospital ships to Southeast Asia. She was one of the first appointees to the board of the American Film Institute, and she has wined and dined with the rulers of Europe and Asia and exchanged ideas with world leaders. She is one of the most fascinating, most vibrant, most liberated women of our times.

There was a time when Shirley MacLaine's life was simpler, slower. She was born April 24, 1934, in Richmond, Virginia, into a family she describes as "decidedly strict middle-class Southern Baptist." Her parents, Ira O. Beaty and Kathlyn MacLean, still alive in Arlington, Virginia. They admit that they don't see Shirley or her brother Warren Beatty much. "But when Shirley comes around," says Mrs. Beaty, "I feel ten years younger."

It seems a miracle that Shirley and Warren broke out of such a traditional, conservative background. Jonas Halperin, an executive at Warner Bros., who's known Shirley for many years, comments, "You have a Shirley MacLaine and a Warren Beatty, who've come out of the womb of a family that is as Wonder Bread and Velveeta cheese and gingham dress and as Middle America and Protestant as you can believe. Someplace in nature, in the creation of chromosomes and genes, this Virginia family delivered two people who totally have no relation to that family." These people are "Down-home folks. Shirley calls them terminal Protestants."

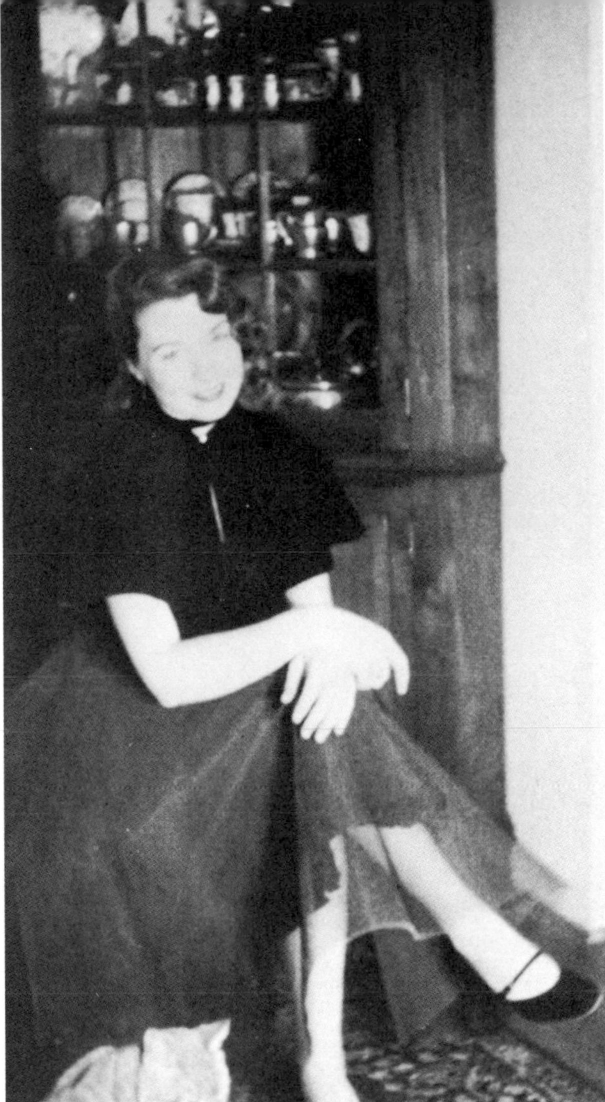

By the late 1940s, Shirley had passed the awkward tomboy stage and had emerged as a lovely young teenager.

On the other hand, Shirley recalls, "My parents entered me in dancing school because I had weak ankles. But once I heard dance music, nobody had to make me go to dancing school. I really loved it. Father is a real estate man, but he had been a band leader before he married mother, and mother had been an actress in Toronto and had taught dramatics at Maryland College. I guess I inherited show-business blood from the both of them, but if I have a sense of rhythm, I got it from my dad."

Shirley made her "debut" singing "Flat Foot Floogie with the Floy Floy" to a neighbor-

Shirley hams it up in full coat, feathered hat, and pants.

hood audience at age three, the same year she began dance school. It also occurred that year that "a fellow companion in rebellion and adjustment entered my life," recalls Shirley, referring to her brother, Warren, born March 30, 1937.

The adults called him Little Henry, because "Warren looked like a character out of the comics. Warren and I have been friends since he was born. I used to punch out anyone who threatened him when he was little. I would have expired down there in Virginia if it hadn't been for him."

When Shirley was four, she did a number called "An Apple for the Teacher" at the Mosque Theatre in Richmond. During her rendition she tripped on the curtain and "the audience laughed," remembers Shirley, "and little ham that I was, I ate it up. After that, I tripped on that curtain every time I passed it."

At age eleven, Shirley and her family moved north to Arlington, Virginia. Freckle-faced and gangly, Shirley was a tomboy with a powerhouse right and a .425 batting average on the local all-boy baseball team. But she continued her dance lessons at the Washington School of Ballet, under the watchful professional eyes of Lisa Gardiner, who had worked with Pavlova, and Mary Day.

A typical day for Shirley began with a 6:00 A.M. wake-up. Breakfast and long bus ride to school. School from 8:30 to 4:30. During the one-and-a-half-hour bus ride into Washington, she did her homework and gobbled her dinner out of a paper bag. Then dance lessons till 7:30, followed by practice and rehearsal till midnight. Back home to Arlington by bus and in bed by 1:30. She sometimes had nightmares that were always the same: "Night after night I'd miss the bus."

Shirley attended Washington-Lee High School in Arlington. She also took singing lessons and learned to play piano, trombone, flute, and violin, gradually phasing out of sports. "I had to give up baseball because I kept slamming more home runs than the boys."

The tallest person in her ballet class (at twelve she was already five feet six), she was often assigned the male roles. She performed in *Hansel and Gretel, The Wizard of Oz, The Nutcracker,* and *Cinderella.* Many of her ballets were presented by the National Symphony Orchestra at Constitution Hall in Washington.

At sixteen, she danced the Fairy Godmother in *Cinderella,* through a two-and-one-half-hour performance, with a broken ankle. An ambulance brought her home, and "I didn't walk for

Probably Shirley's first "cheesecake" photo, wherein she displays her 34-24-34 proportions.

Shirley smiles approvingly as crew-cut brother Warren shows off his early ambition to be a composer.

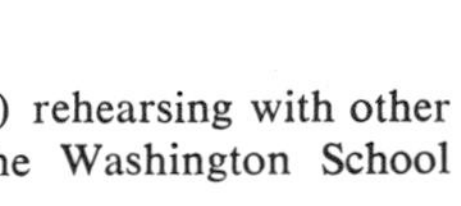

Shirley (center) rehearsing with other members of the Washington School of Ballet.

On the set of *The Trouble with Harry* in Vermont, October 12, 1954, Shirley displays her best pixie face.

four months," Shirley remembers. While recuperating, Shirley decided she would go to New York City for advanced ballet studies. During her 1950 summer hiatus she got a job in the chorus line of *Oklahoma!* at the City center.

Though invited to the Berlin Arts Festival along with the rest of the cast after the New York run of *Oklahoma!* was over, Shirley decided to return home and finish high school, before launching her second assault on the New York theater world when she was eighteen.

As she stated in her autobiography, *Don't Fall Off the Mountain,* "I arrived in New York at eighteen, wide-eyed, optimistic, brave, and certain I would crash the world of show business overnight. Naïveté is a necessary personality trait in order to endure New York, and a masochistic sense of humor an indispensable quirk."

Shirley plunked down sixty-four dollars for the first month's rent on a fifth-floor walkup apartment at the southern tip of Harlem, at 116th street and Broadway. "The building was crawling with dope addicts," Shirley recalls. When she complained to her landlord that the multitudinous cockroaches and bedbugs prevented her from sleeping, she was told to plug her ears and keep her mouth shut.

With no financial support from her parents,

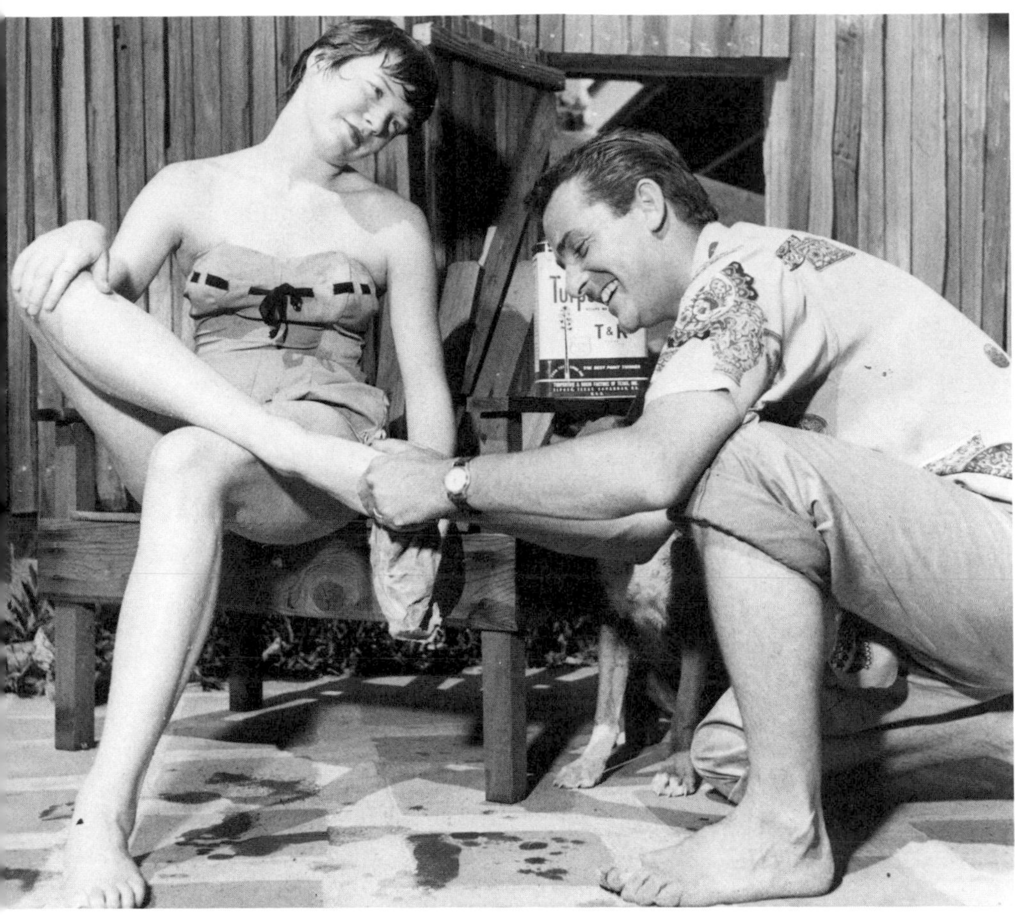

Husband Steve Parker dries Shirley's feet on the porch of their beach house at Malibu, California, 1955.

she survived on savings from *Oklahoma!* and baby-sitting money. Waiting for her first job, she spent most of her money on dance lessons. What little was left she often spent at the Automat. For nearly a year, Shirley's diet consisted mainly of peanut-butter sandwiches on raisin bread, washed down by lemonade she made from lemon wedges, water, and sugar, which were all free.

In the summer of 1952, Shirley landed a job in the chorus of *Kiss Me Kate* at St. John Terrell's Music Circus in Lambertsville, New Jersey. That fall, she auditioned and won a job on the road circuit of the Servel Ice Box trade show. As the Queen of Swans, Shirley's routine called for her to do fifty-five consecutive turns around the refrigerator while it churned out ice. Enough turns, Shirley remembers, "to whip the cream in the box if I'd been geared to it."

After six months of twirling to the strains of *Swan Lake,* Shirley did her last performance with a saintly smile and two blacked-out front teeth. For this indiscretion she was promptly fired. She returned to New York in time to audition for Rodgers and Hammerstein's new musical, *Me and Juliet.*

Turned down twice, she remembers, "The third time was my lucky one." Richard Rodgers selected her from all the women onstage by saying, "Hey, you with the legs!" With her new job Shirley also had a new name, MacLaine. Until then people had had trouble pronouncing Beaty (Bay-tee), so she adopted her mother's maiden name with altered spelling.

Me and Juliet opened in May 1953 at the Majestic Theatre and ran 358 performances. One evening after dancing in the chorus Shirley met William T. (Steve) Parker, introduced by a woman friend.

The rugged-looking, dark-haired, blue-eyed former paratrooper was an actor, off-Broadway director, and aspiring producer. He was also twelve years her senior. They met in a bar on West 45th Street in Manhattan. Shirley got her glass stuck in her mouth while drinking, and

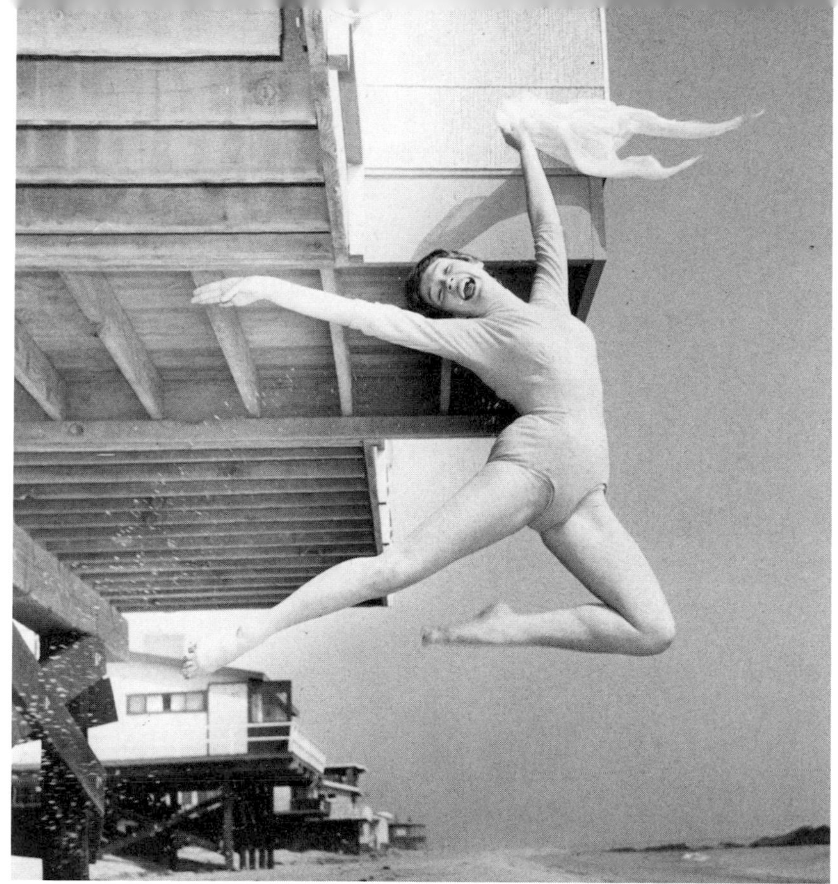

Shirley attempts a grand jeté onto the Malibu beach, 1955.

Parker reached over and pried it loose. She remembers falling in love with him "immediately."

Steve Parker had spent much of his childhood in the Far East. Orphaned at sixteen, he had traveled extensively, working at odd jobs. After Pearl Harbor, he joined the paratroopers. His fluent Japanese was invaluable. A captain by age twenty-two, he was decorated and discharged with honors, after which he returned to America.

So intense was the involvement between MacLaine and Parker from that first moment on, that "we forgot to get married until 1954." Also postponing their marriage was Shirley's new job in the chorus line of *Pajama Game*. The

Shirley and Steve try the water at Malibu, 1955.

Steve and Shirley ponder a magazine in one of her earliest publicity shots.

night before the New York opening on May 9, 1954, Shirley was made understudy to the female lead, Carol Haney.

As Shirley recalls it in her autobiography: "Only four days after the opening and already I was depressed. I was in another hit! More weekly paychecks, enervating security and monotony." That evening, a downtrodden Shirley arrived at the stage door, where a frantic Hal Prince, the show's producer, blurted out that Carol Haney had broken her ankle and that unrehearsed Shirley was "on right now!"

Fatefully, Shirley had brought her termination notice in her hand. She quickly shoved it back into her purse. Co-star John Raitt was forced to sing her first-act song, *Hernando's Hideaway,* because Shirley didn't know the lyrics. The second act opened with the much-noted dance routine, *Steam Heat.* This song and dance for a trio of two men and one woman called for a derby to be tossed, tumbled, and juggled throughout the number.

Shirley's worst fear became a reality when she dropped the derby and said, "Shit!" loudly enough to be heard through the first several rows. She quickly retrieved her derby and

Shirley and Steve relax by the fireplace in their little beach house, 1955.

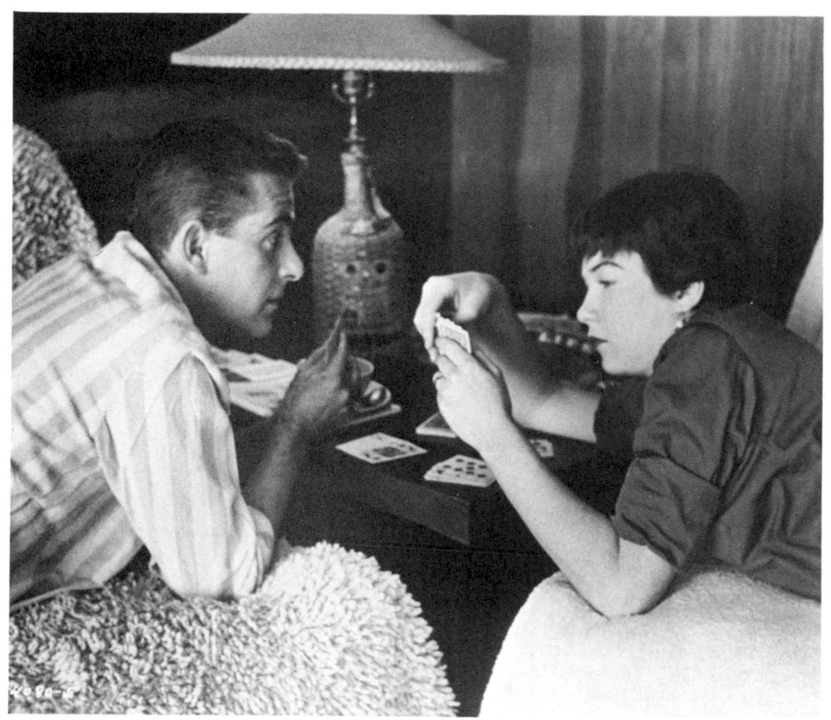

Steve and Shirley play cards in their beach house filled with makeshift furniture, 1955.

shrugged "a sort of apology to the audience." When the curtain calls came, the same audience that had booed when learning Haney would be replaced, now stood up and cheered.

This was the turning point in her career. She had now discovered her individuality as a performer. Steve congratulated her in the dressing room, saying, "You were great. But you still have a long way to go." Shirley knew he meant that since she was now a "star," a higher level of struggle was necessary.

The third night Shirley went on as Haney's substitute, Paramount Pictures' highly successful independent executive producer Hal Wallis was in the audience. After the final curtain, Wallis came backstage with an offer to meet Shirley and discuss her future. A screen test was arranged for at Fox-Movietone in New York. "When I made the screen test," Shirley recalls laughingly, "I had a hole in my tights."

The seven-year contract she signed with Wallis called for her services in Hollywood in December of 1954. It was then only May. Three months later, Doc Ericson, Paramount production manager, and Herbie Coleman, associate producer for Alfred Hitchcock, were in the audience and saw Shirley substituting for then laryngitis-ridden Carol Haney. Coleman met Shirley backstage after the show and talked to her about Hitchcock's newest picture-to-be, a macabre comedy called *The Trouble with Harry.*

Hitchcock was in New York staying at the St. Regis Hotel. He called Shirley and invited her to his suite to discuss a possible deal. Upon her arrival, Hitchcock asked Shirley what motion pictures she had done, what television shows she had guested on, and what speaking roles she had done on Broadway. She replied to all three questions that she had no professional acting experience.

Hitchcock told her that she must be the color of shamrock, to which she agreed. Unperturbed, Hitchcock said, "All this simply means is that I shall have fewer bad knots to untie. You're hired."

Told to report to Vermont in three days to begin filming, Shirley readied a wardrobe Hitchcock had approved and informed everyone that she was leaving.

On September 17, 1954, between the matinee and evening performances of *Pajama Game,* Shirley and Steve were married at the Marble Collegiate Church, with Dr. Norman Vincent Peale officiating. The next day they were on

Shirley relaxes on the porch of her beach house.

their way to Vermont for location shooting.

Shirley's contract with Wallis provided for loanouts to other studios and for five television appearances per year. Of course, the contract favored Wallis, since it enabled him to reap a large share of whatever money was paid to his client. He had "discovered" and developed such stars as Dean Martin and Jerry Lewis, Burt Lancaster, Kirk Douglas, Lizabeth Scott, Shirley Booth, and Charlton Heston. Shirley, as it has turned out, was to be just about the last big Hollywood star to be churned out from this old Hollywood studio system.

The loanout was made with ease, since Wallis and Hitchcock both worked out of the same studio at that time. Shirley and Steve arrived in Hollywood to finish interiors for *The Trouble with Harry*. They bought a second-hand green Buick and drove to the beach at Malibu where they rented a one-room "shack," built on pilings that shook each time a wave rolled in.

Shortly thereafter, Steve and Shirley were involved in a bad auto accident that left Shirley in a neck brace for a month and Steve in the hospital with severe lacerations and a slipped disc. Wallis gave them a belated wedding gift, a sporty MG roadster, which Shirley quickly learned to drive to and from the studio each day.

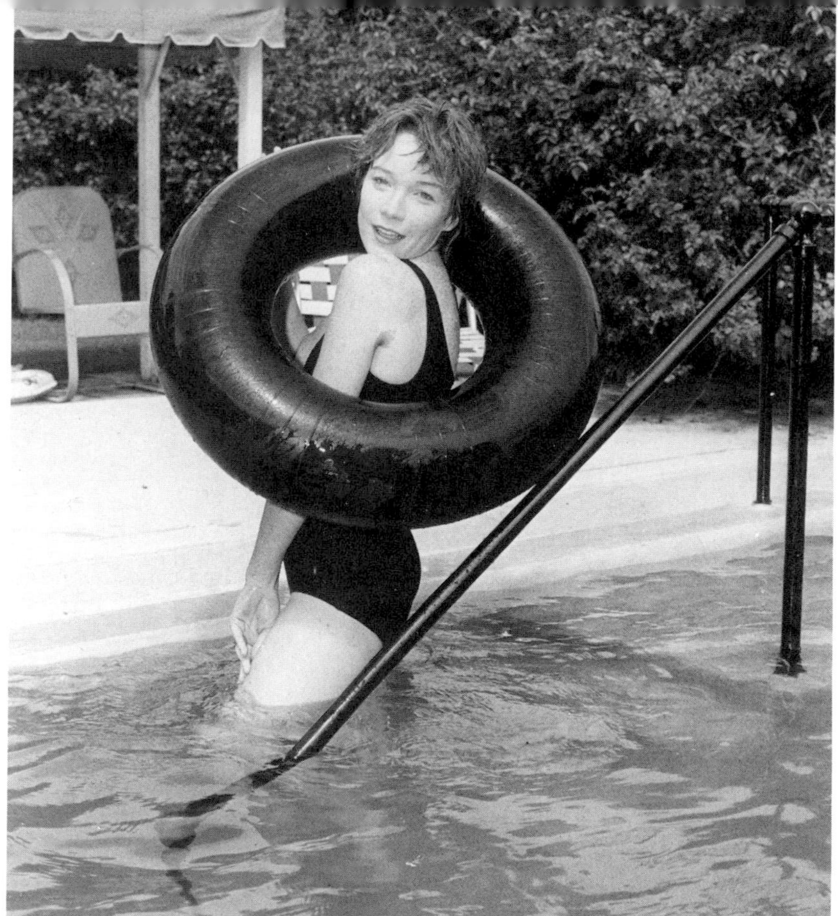

Shirley poses most unglamorously with an inner tube, in a pool in Hollywood, 1959.

The Trouble with Harry received excellent critical notices but could stir no domestic box-office business, though it fared quite well in Europe and did smashingly in the Far East, where according to Shirley, "it is considered hilarious to deal with death." The critics had only good things to say about Shirley, and Hitchcock remarked that he thought Shirley "a great dramatic actress."

The fan magazines and gossip columnists quickly labeled Shirley a kook, because she neither looked nor dressed nor acted like any of the ingenues then in vogue, like Natalie Wood. Billy Wilder, who later directed her in *The Apartment,* said of Shirley's attitude toward dress, "By her own admission, Shirley is one of the worst dressers alive. Her clothes are unbelievably bizarre. But clothes just don't mean that much to her, nor do furs or jewelry. She would wear Eskimo shoes and a hula skirt if it would amuse her."

Since she was five feet, six and a half inches tall, weighing 118 pounds, with pixie-cut wild red hair, blue eyes, and a map of Ireland for a face, plus a 34-24-34 figure with legs up to her shoulders, publicists were hard put to come up with a sultry or girl-next-door image that the public would buy. Paramount and Wallis tried to transform her into Miss Hollywood Starlet. Shirley was none too cooperative—they never quite succeeded.

Wallis wasted no time using Shirley to garnish his newest Dean Martin–Jerry Lewis production, *Artists and Models*. Shirley had no artistic control at this time, and she thought of her role (a hussy who ran up and down stairs chasing Dean and Jerry) as a shallow one. She felt she represented "all the plain broads" in the audience who could never get a man unless they sat on him and held him down. And in one scene, that is exactly what she did to Jerry in order to force a marriage proposal out of him. "I hated that," she later remarked.

The critics, however, were disarmed by her naturalness and zany flair for comedy. And though she disliked the picture, she enjoyed working with Martin and Lewis. She said of Lewis, "I think he is a real genius; he taught me so much and was so patient."

Though they had been married only a short time, Shirley's union with Steve took a radical turn. Parker has confessed, "I felt like a second-class citizen. I was beginning to be called Mr. MacLaine. It was a situation I could not accept."

Shirley receives a visit from her husband, Steve Parker, on the set of *Can-Can* in September 1959.

Realizing it would be impossible to lose that stigma in Hollywood, Parker decided he would return to Japan to work as a theatrical producer. With his extensive knowledge of the people and their customs, he reckoned he could make a fine liaison with Western companies that were just then beginning to expand wholeheartedly into the Far East.

In 1955, Mike Todd offered Shirley a role in *Around the World in 80 Days,* to be filmed partly in Japan. She leaped at the offer, knowing it would reunite her with Steve. In fact, she became pregnant in Japan (an accident, she called it later) and later returned to Hollywood to have her baby.

Steve went to Hollywood for the birth but soon informed Shirley that business would force him back to Japan before the birth. That was August 31, 1956. Shirley rushed to the hospital and informed the doctors that she wanted to have her baby immediately. They induced labor, and on September 1, 1956, Shirley presented Steve with their first and only child, a six-pound daughter, Stephanie Sachiko Parker.

Parker had told Shirley that when he was serving in the U.S. army in Japan, there were thousands of children who were starving and homeless. One little girl in particular crept into his heart and was adopted by his group. They called her Sachiko, which means happy child in Japanese, and Parker had made formal applications to adopt her, when she died of tuberculosis. He then decided if he ever had a daughter he would name her Sachiko.

After moving his family to larger quarters, Parker returned to Japan, and Shirley remained in Hollywood with Sachie. During her pregnancy, Shirley had amended her contract with Wallis. As of March 1956, she would receive six thousand dollars per picture during the first period (comprising two films), seventy-five hundred in the second, ten thousand in the third, fifteen thousand in the fourth, and twenty thousand in the fifth. Wallis would exercise his third option on Shirley's contract in early 1959. Shirley referred to these years under Wallis as "my white-slave-contract days."

Showman-producer extraordinaire Mike Todd's extravaganza *Around the World in 80 Days* broke all existing box-office records by grossing twenty million dollars during its first domestic release; yet it did nothing to boost Shirley's career. Though she had feverishly practiced an English accent to be used in the film, Todd had her voice overdubbed at the last minute. She was caught playing the straight role to the rest of the cast's grand caricatures, and her performance was lost. Back in Hollywood her career slowed to a creak.

She quickly accepted the female lead on stage in Terence Rattigan's *The Sleeping Prince* (later filmed as *The Prince and the Showgirl* with Marilyn Monroe in Shirley's part). It bombed in Los Angeles but made money in San Francisco; Shirley received fine notices in both cities. Said *Variety,* "A triumph for Miss MacLaine, it stamps her as a bright comedy talent, combining perception and variation to create a character that lives and sparkles."

Her good notices aroused Wallis's interest in her again, and he immediately cast her in two new films at Paramount, *The Matchmaker* and *Hot Spell.* He also loaned her to MGM for a handsome sum for three upcoming features, *The Sheepman, Some Came Running,* and *Ask Any Girl.*

1957 and 1958 saw Shirley exercising her option to do TV work. She appeared on "The Dinah Shore Chevy Show" and showed millions across America how well she could sing, dance, and improvise. In 1958, she signed a three-year deal with NBC for five hundred thousand dollars, calling for fifteen guest appearances.

The Sheepman opened in the spring of 1958 to a quiet box office. Shirley recalled, "I was the only gal in the picture. Director George Marshall threw a couple of fistfuls of dirt all over my new clothes. In the first minute all of them [the cast] knocked me down, rolled me in the dirt and said, 'O.K., now you can play a western.'" A moment later Shirley doused her tormentors with a bucket of water. "Wouldn't you like to cool off?" she quipped. "From then on they knew I wasn't a prima donna exactly, and whatever they wanted to say they went right ahead." Even Shirley, who's been known to exercise the English language with the ardor of a longshoreman, said of Marshall and her co-stars, "Their lan-

Shirley rehearses a strenuous dance routine for *Can-Can* in 1959.

guage, oh golly!" Again, the critics approved of her performance.

Shirley said the role of the hard-boiled cowgirl was the real MacLaine. Performing in a work shirt and jeans reminded her of how she dressed at home. The public warmed to her again and enjoyed once more the naturalness of her performance.

With Parker now mostly in Japan and Shirley at home in Hollywood, she became the brunt of much negative publicity. Parker thought of his family as "an international family of the future, speaking several languages, having several businesses and homes in different countries." But his concepts were well ahead of the times.

In *McCall's* in 1976, Shirley said she did not want to change her marriage. She had the "perfect marriage," she said. "He lives on one side of the world, and I live on the other, and we can sleep with whomever we choose." She wasn't looking for a divorce to wed her closest companion, author Pete Hamill. She insists she'll never marry again.

Shirley followed *The Sheepman* with *The Matchmaker,* co-starring Shirley Booth, Tony Perkins, and Robert Morse. She found working with Shirley Booth to be a drama lesson in itself. Shirley called the finished film "a romp. It's hilarious!"

Shirley teamed again with Shirley Booth for *Hot Spell,* directed by Daniel Mann, who had directed her first screen test. Shirley was third-billed, behind Booth and Anthony Quinn. Once more, the critics were enthusiastic.

Shirley remembers those years, with the gossip about her, as a difficult time. "I learned a lot about life just by deciphering the filthy shades of meaning that filled the gossip. I was an enigma. I intrigued them. They didn't have a pigeonhole for me." But the gossipers were right about one thing, Shirley admits: "I was desperately lonely."

Her career was then shot into high gear by the film *Some Came Running.* It made her into a full-fledged star in the grandest Hollywood tradition. Recalls Shirley, *"Some Came Running*

Shirley, with the rest of the cast and the crew of *Can-Can,* poses with Soviet Premier Khrushchev during his famous visit to the set of the film.

Shirley and her "discoverer," powerful producer Hal Wallis, smiling together on the set of *All in a Night's Work,* 1960.

was the turning point in my film career. It was Frank Sinatra who swung me the picture, by killing me off—a good death scene is always good theater."

Director Vincente Minnelli and Frank Sinatra had seen Shirley on "The Dinah Shore Chevy Show" dancing in black leotards and belting out a song off-key. Instantly they agreed she was the Ginny Moorhead they were looking for. By now, Shirley's agent was the giant Music Corporation of America. They demanded for her all the $75,000 MGM had offered, and Wallis, of course, wanted her to take $10,600, as called for in their contract. Shirley, feeling this role was crucial to her career, finally convinced MCA to agree with Wallis.

The film was a major success for all. It made more than four million dollars in the United States alone. Shirley garnered her first Oscar nomination for Best Actress, later losing to Susan Hayward for *I Want to Live.*

During the filming on location in Indiana, Shirley became part of what the press dubbed the Clan, headed by Frank Sinatra. Shirley was the only female allowed to enter the inner circle of Frank, Dean Martin, Sammy Davis, Jr., and Peter Lawford. She was the mascot. They all stayed in the same house and taught Shirley how to cheat at gin as well as all sorts of cinema tricks of the trade. "We used to go to Vegas every twenty minutes," Shirley recalls, "and turn it upside-down."

No one, Shirley remembers, ever made an overture to her during the filming, nor did they ever question her about her personal life. She was always looked after and protected by the Clan. "If anyone approached me," said Shirley, "one of them always stepped in front of me."

Dean Martin said at the time of the film, "We all respect her as a married woman and that's it. We kid around, we hug her, but that's all."

Director Billy Wilder clowns with Shirley on the set of *The Apartment* between takes, 1960.

Sinatra chimed in, "That's the truth, though a lot of people hate to believe it. But it's a good thing Shirl doesn't worry what other people think about her." He later elaborated on this relationship with Shirley, revealing, "We have a kind of trust in each other. If Shirley tells me to read a book, I read it. I trust her taste and knowledge, and I think she trusts mine. She is a kind of a kook but very warm."

Shirley was still searching for herself at this time. "When I first came here," she told columnist Sidney Skolsky, "I was filled with the success drive, because I really didn't feel I had any talent." Shirley had been in and out of psychotherapy since 1955. "I wanted to know more about me. I was subject to depression, and the adjustment to success wasn't easy. I was used to fighting to do better, and Hollywood just seemed to be interested in selling me."

Her next film, released in 1959, was *Ask Any Girl,* which won Shirley the Silver Bear Award at the Berlin Film Festival as Best Actress in a Foreign Film. That year she also won the British Academy Award for Best Foreign Actress. In it she was again teamed with David Niven, who remembered her fondly from the days of their first film together, *Around the World in 80 Days.* "She was a lovely, fresh, unspoiled young woman with a lively sense of humor and a strong sense of dignity. I really didn't think that with her kind of sensitivity, she would survive in Hollywood."

Career was her next film, but it did not prove as rewarding. Her portrayal of a good-natured tramp lacked the sympathy and pathos of Ginny Moorhead. Though the critics were lukewarm to her performance, director Joseph Anthony said, "She has great inner reality. She's a method actress. It's entirely sensory; she doesn't like to intellectualize."

As her reputation grew as an actress, so did a tolerance toward her unconventional life-style. The gossip mills ground out less and less offensive material. The old guard was dying away, as was the studio system itself.

Shirley did a quick cameo for pal Frank Sinatra in his 1960 crime caper, *Ocean's 11.* She had a twenty-second-long scene as a drunk in a casino bar, unbilled in the credits.

The lavish six-million-dollar production of

Can-Can followed, with its now famous story of Premier Nikita Khrushchev's visit to the set and his nasty comments later. When Shirley heard that Khrushchev was coming to the set, she took a crash course in Russian. She made a speech in his own tongue welcoming him and subsequently received dozens of irate letters accusing her of pandering to the Russian dictator.

Shirley told the *Saturday Evening Post* that Khrushchev "seemed to like it very much. He smiled throughout the whole performance; yet he complained afterward that it had been too risqué. I don't think that Mrs. Khrushchev liked even our comparatively modest costumes. She wasn't smiling, and I think Mr. Khrushchev began to disapprove after he saw the frown on Mama's face." *Can-Can* was not well liked by the critics, but the public went anyway. Shirley followed that with Billy Wilder's film *The Apartment,* for which she received her second Oscar nomination. When she lost to Elizabeth Taylor in the Oscar race, Billy Wilder sent Shirley a wire saying that he loved her even if she didn't have a hole in her windpipe. (Many agree that Taylor won on a sympathy vote because of her near fatal illness that year.) "I understand Elizabeth Taylor was furious about that," he says.

The famous gin-game sequence in *The Apartment* was especially written in by Wilder, because Shirley was always playing gin on the set between takes. Shirley never needed to study scripts, being blessed with a photographic memory. One quick scan, and she had her lines down pat.

When not filming, Shirley led the life of a bachelor mother, looking after Sachi. Even after twelve hours at the studio, Shirley, who requires only four to five hours' sleep per night, would often bundle Sachi up into a small wicker hamper and head out for a party. Once there, Shirley would find a dark, quiet place for Sachi to sleep, stash her, then join the party.

Shirley makes merry with pal Donald O'Connor backstage at one of his shows in Las Vegas in the early 1960s.

Robert Mitchum, director Robert Wise, and Shirley pose during a break from filming *Two for the Seesaw,* 1962.

Shirley attempted to explain her behavior to *McCall's* back then: "I wanted Steffie to go wherever I went. I wanted her to know that the way Steve and I live was the way she had to live too. She had to get used to traveling and sleeping in all kinds of crazy places with all kinds of crazy noise going on. She had to get used to being with Daddy, with Mommy not around, then suddenly having to leave Daddy to be alone with Mommy."

On international flights between Hollywood and Japan, Sachi became an adored mascot of the airline crews, always quiet and well behaved, and after a few trips to the Far East, she was multilingual. After age seven, Sachi went to Japan to live full-time with her father. After age twelve, she chose to attend a boarding school in Switzerland. During those years, Sachie would return to spend Easter, Christmas, and summers with her mother. After boarding school Sachie attended college, studying in Australia and Hawaii, where she is now settled.

As assertive as Shirley is on most subjects, she has some doubts when she talks about Sachie. "There were times when I felt I should be more of a conventional mother," she told the *Washington Post.* "And then I'd talk to Sachie about it, and she'd say, 'No, I think what you're doing is right."

Today, Shirley insists, "We have a good relationship. Sachie is a very wise young woman and a serious Oriental scholar. Our times together mean a lot to both of us." Sachie assures her mother she's glad she had the opportunity to achieve her identity on her own and earlier than many of her peers.

In 1961, Shirley was back co-starring with Dean Martin for the fifth time in *All in a Night's Work.* Though in it she returned to the redheaded, frantic hoyden role of her earlier years, it was a place for her to hone her comic gifts. The critics praised her and Martin.

Shirley's next outing is less well remembered. In *Two Loves,* with Laurence Harvey and Jack Hawkins, she is miscast as a frigid schoolmarm fighting off the advances of a would-be lover Harvey. The original story line, from an excellent novel by Sylvia Ashton-Warner, is all but lost. The color photography of Joseph Ruttenberg is the true star here.

"When I worked with Audrey Hepburn in *The Children's Hour,* recalls Shirley, "she taught me how to dress and I taught her how to cuss!"

Director William Wyler, a perfectionist task-

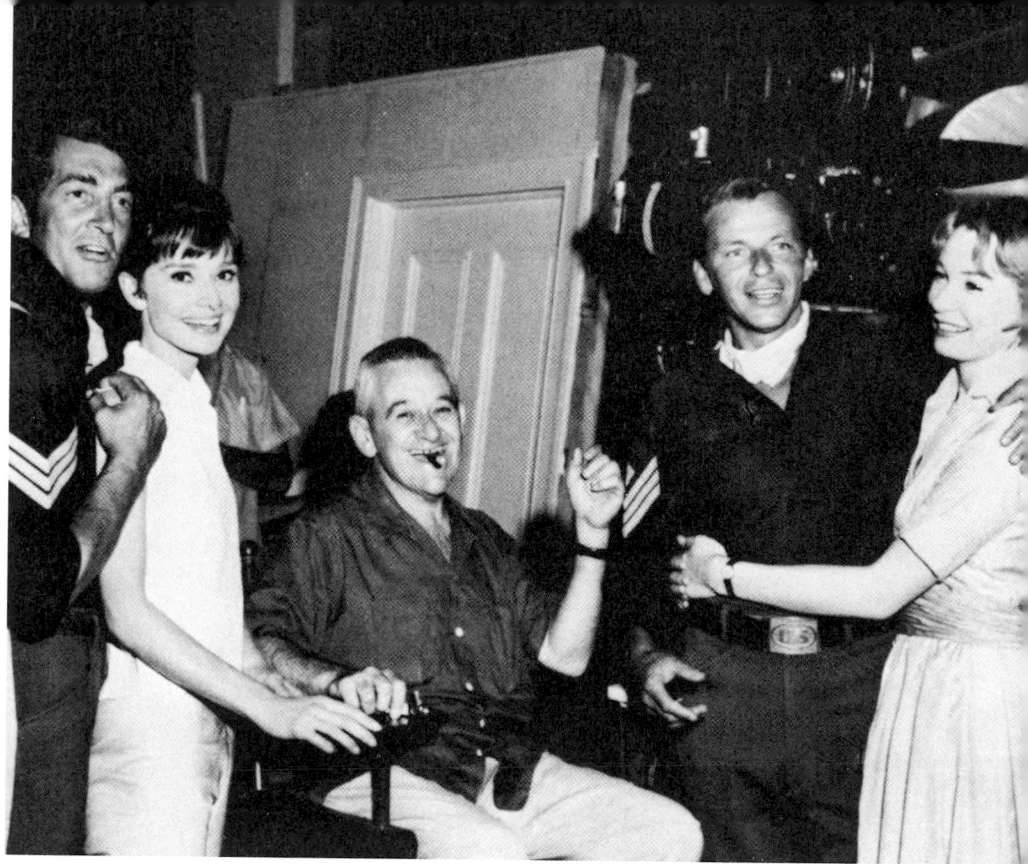

Shirley receives a visit from pals Dean Martin and Frank Sinatra on the set of *The Children's Hour*. Audrey Hepburn and director William Wyler share her delight.

master, said in his biography, "Audrey like most actresses will require a moment to get herself in the proper mood for the scene, but Shirley—she will make jokes and clown it up until the last possible second and then, when the camera starts she will be right in it." Shirley feels many of her best scenes were cut because Wyler was afraid of being too open about the Lesbian-suicide story. The reviews were mixed, but Shirley received some fine notices for her performance as it stood.

During her nine years under Hal Wallis, he had made millions off her on loan-outs while Shirley averaged $15,800 per picture. She sued Wallis under the California labor laws, but days before the trial she settled out of court, paying Wallis $150,000 and freeing herself from any further obligations.

The thing most worth noting about *My Geisha,* besides the fact it was shot in Japan and produced by her husband, Steve, was Shirley's research for the part. She lived for two weeks in the Gion Caburenjo (geisha training school), where she learned the intricacies of the delicate tea ceremony, how to play the stringed instrument called samisen, and the art of Japanese dance. No Westerner had ever been allowed into such a training school before, much less lived in one for any length of time.

The better part of a chapter in the autobiography of the famed Westmore makeup-artist family is devoted to the immense and painful complexities of Shirley's makeup for *My Geisha.* At times she wore a black Geisha wig weighing more than twenty pounds. Painful plastic tabs were employed to pull back her eyes, to ensure the Oriental look. And finally, she was fitted with brown contact lenses that caused her eyes to tear interminably. It was a pain-filled but fascinating experience for all, though not well received by the critics.

The experience of *My Geisha* was not always painful for Shirley. There was plenty of levity on the set, mostly at the expense of co-star Yves Montand. Montand had his own version of the English language. Early on, Montand told MacLaine he'd rather not cope with our difficult language too early in the morning. "I sleep in French," he explained, "and English gives me a headache too soon after breakfast." After a fine Japanese dinner, he said it was "the best meal I ever met." To MacLaine's observation that he spoke English with a southern-Japanese accent, Montand replied, "You pull my legs."

During her bout with Wallis, Shirley, known in the early days for having a short fuse, had a run-in with *Hollywood Reporter* columnist

Director Bob Fosse guides Shirley through a dance routine during a rehearsal for *Sweet Charity,* 1968.

Mike Connolly. Over the years Connolly had written, as Shirley said in her first book, "that I had tried to commit suicide over an unhappy affair and intimated strongly that on another of my trips I had had an abortion." The straw that broke the camel's back was when Connolly reported Shirley had lost her suit against Hal Wallis. Infuriated, Shirley confronted Connolly in his office and delivered to his face two open-handed powerhouse right hooks. Shortly thereafter Shirley received a wire from President Kennedy saying:

> DEAR SHIRLEY—CONGRATULATIONS ON YOUR FIGHT STOP NOW IF YOU HAD REAL GUTS YOU'D SLUG WALLACE—GOVERNOR NOT HAL. JFK

In 1963, Shirley took second billing to Jack Lemmon in *Irma la Douce,* directed by Billy Wilder. The story of the hooker with the heart of gold grossed twelve million dollars in domestic rentals alone. *Irma la Douce* had such an impact on the public that when Shirley would walk down the via Veneto in Rome, people used to call out, "Irma la Douce, how much you charge?"

Shirley raised eyebrows because her research consisted in following a real prostitute through her rounds in the red-light district of Paris.

In the original print of *Irma la Douce,* Jack Lemmon looks at Shirley naked in a bathtub through the wrong end of a telescope. He therefore sees a very small, though naked, image. When the rushes were first shown in Hollywood, the picture was blown up. "And there I was," explained Shirley, "without a thing on, up on the screen. Some of my friends were naturally giggling. I couldn't tell them, 'No, no, they're not going to show that much of me in the picture . . . it's going to be real small.'

"Honest," said Shirley, "I watched the

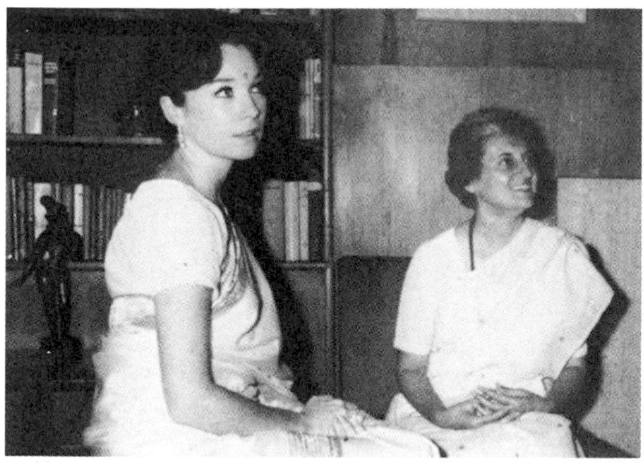

Shirley, dressed in traditional Indian sari, chats with then prime minister of India, Indira Gandhi, in New Delhi, 1967.

whole thing with my head turned the other way. And when they showed me the still prints—I made a bonfire of the whole thing."

With *Irma la Douce* came Shirley's third Oscar nomination for Best Actress. *Film Daily* named her Actress of the Year. Grauman's Chinese Theater had her plant her hand prints, and she won the Golden Globe from the Foreign Press Association. She also trekked to Harvard that year to accept their Hasty Pudding Award, to which she quipped, "I'm sorry I didn't go to college. I would like to be educated. But it's too late. I'm a millionaire."

By her early thirties this was true. She is an excellent businesswoman. Wise investments, especially in property, foreign and domestic, plus

Shirley spent one month living with the fierce Masai warrior tribe in East Africa. They made her a blood sister. The fascinated children followed her everywhere.

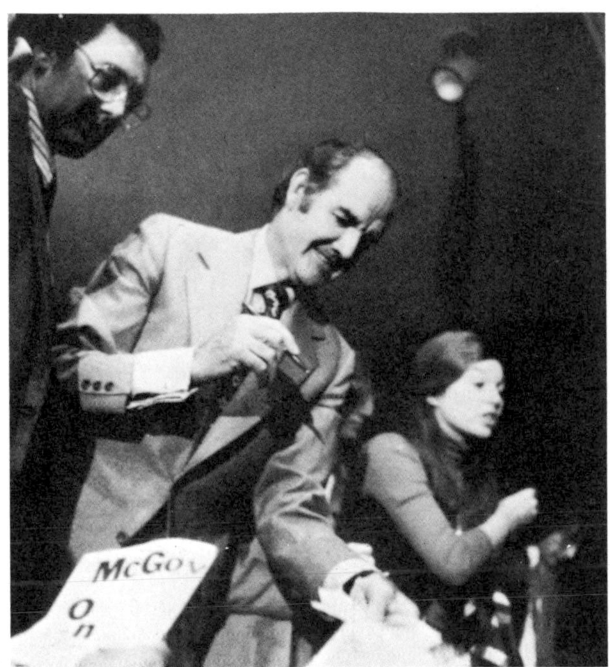

In 1972, Shirley campaigned for one long year, traveling all over the country for Senator George McGovern's presidential race. She was a delegate to the Democratic National Convention.

percentages of her films (she owned 10 percent of *Irma la Douce*) and an eight-hundred-thousand-dollar-per-film fee made her independently wealthy quite early. At this time Shirley was also spending two hundred thousand dollars a year on travel expenses for her family and about six thousand to ten thousand dollars on phone calls to Sachi and Steve in Japan.

Being a star became quite a responsibility. In 1962 she told *Good Housekeeping* that she felt she was in "constant battle with all the people I pay to protect and advise me." Her people kept reminding her, "It doesn't befit a star to do this or that." But, Shirley replied, "I'm the one who has to lick the problem of remaining a human being in this rat race. I have to be what I am."

In 1964, Shirley was in the top ten at the box office. Her first release that year was *What a Way to Go!* A farce, it did poorly and died quickly. Even the likes of co-stars Paul Newman and Robert Mitchum couldn't save the soggy script. Besides the endless clothing changes required by the seventy-plus costumes designed by Edith Head, Shirley found her role "was very difficult because I had to adjust to a different male star every few weeks."

If anything, the *What a Way to Go!* experience was preparation for the fiasco that was *John Goldfarb, Please Come Home.* Surely the low point in her career, it had an inane script by William Peter Blatty based on the Francis Gary Powers U-2 spy incident. "What a movie!" Shirley told *Sports Illustrated.* "A dumb broad runs through the whole Notre Dame football team. *Goldfarb* sank into inanity." Enough said.

In Shirley's vignette in 1965's *The Yellow Rolls-Royce,* she co-starred with George C. Scott, Alain Delon, and Art Carney. Handsomely mounted in Europe, the film made bundles of money. The critics were not so impressed with the content, but Shirley scored a personal hit with the film crew in Italy. When she and Delon finished their love scenes the Italian extras and crew broke into applause. The Italians explained that for two people who weren't Italian they had really put a lot into their clinches.

Gambit was a movie with a first quarter that "didn't work because of the dialogue," Shirley recalls. She asked, "Why don't we do it without dialogue, like it's a dream?" That's exactly what the producers did, and she didn't have to learn any lines for the first three weeks. She got to like her co-star, Michael Caine, "a darling, a sweetheart, and very originally funny." *Gambit* was Caine's first American movie, and he used to tell Shirley who he had been out with the night before and whether she wore panty hose or a girdle and whether he could get them off.

She says she likes Englishmen because they are "a little reserved, and they like someone who's a little bawdy."

If the beginnings of a decline in Shirley's career started with *Goldfarb* and *What a Way to Go, Gambit* was only a a temporary reprieve. *Woman Times Seven* was to put the proverbial icing on the cake.

At first it all sounded great. Recalls Shirley, "De Sica phoned me saying he'd been waiting ten years to make this film but hadn't found an actress capable of playing seven roles. I told him I wasn't sure he'd found her yet. I made myself a piece of putty and let him do what he wanted with me."

Shirley's statement was rather prophetic; most critics agreed her talents were not up to the demands of this multiple role. Shirley walked

Shirley and former co-star Gene Kelly smile for the photogs in this shot from the early 1970s.

away with fifty-six thousand dollars for fifteen weeks, courtesy Joe Levine, but received no percentage of the profits, since the film committed the cardinal sin of the movie industry by making no money.

Despite *Woman Times Seven*'s fizzling at the box office, there was a small redemption for Shirley in 1967, when she was named Best Actress of the Year by the National Association of Theatre Owners. Paul Newman copped the Best Actor award and shared the dais with Shirley at the ceremony. The old friends from *What a Way to Go!* times laughed and cavorted for the cameras and had a good old time.

With money no object in her personal life (she was, incidentally, $750,000 richer from a suit she had brought against Fox for canceling *Bloomer Girl,* negating their agreement for her to star, in 1965), Shirley took off on a series of personal adventures later chronicled so well in *Don't Fall Off the Mountain.* She visited and lived with the fierce Masai tribe in Africa and was made a blood sister; escaped possible death in a military coup in Bhutan; and worked all through the southern United States in the civil rights movement.

(Shirley recalled that her political awareness had begun in Richmond, as a teenager, "when I realized there was an emotional harshness whenever anyone spoke in bigoted terms.

Niggers smelled bad, Jews had horns, and Catholics wanted to overcome the world with little Catholics. It was revolting.")

One critic called *The Bliss of Mrs. Blossom* (1968) the sleeper of the year. Shirley gave a nicely etched comedic performance, ably supported by Richard Attenborough and James Booth. Poor distribution hurt the film's earning possibilities and Shirley's chance to restore in everyone's eyes her abilities as a fine comedienne. Making the film proved a personally enjoyable experience for the cast; Attenborough remarked of Shirley, "I guess we are all hooked on her."

Sensing that her stock was down in Hollywood, Shirley attacked her starring role in *Sweet Charity* with the fury and determination only she possesses. She began by spending three months of solid dance practice to get in shape, working alone in a studio with director Bob Fosse's then wife, the original Broadway stage Charity, superb actress-dancer Gwen Verdon. It had been twelve years since Shirley had done any serious dancing, and it showed. She quit smoking, went on a special diet, and took singing lessons for months prior to filming.

Bob Fosse knew Shirley well, since he had been the dance director of *Pajama Game* back in 1954. He recalled the Shirley of those days as "a pleasant girl with red hair and freckles, very willing, with a kind of circus in her face. She had a little piece of business, running out of a crowd and kissing the boss at a company party. It always got a roar. I thought, 'Well, it's just a funny piece of business.' Then she left for Hollywood, and they must have tried eight or ten girls doing this stupid little thing, and it died. Then I realized Shirley had something special. What Shirley lacks for not keeping up with her dancing, she makes up in her enthusiasm and drive."

Shirley's playing the easy girl with the heart of gold didn't wash with 1969 audiences. *Sweet Charity* was overlong and overblown; even reduced admission prices couldn't coax audiences

Vaudevillian Sally DeMay and world famous hypnotist-magician Joan Brandon honor Shirley as show-business Trouper of the Year for 1977.

Shirley converses with friends Rock Hudson and Juliet Prowse.

away from television and TV Dinners.

Shirley decided it was time to take a breather. Of course, a breather to Shirley is just switching her immense energies over to other projects, not stopping and relaxing. In her year off she put the finishing touches on her autobiography and got elected as a delegate to the 1968 Democratic National Convention, campaigning for Bobby Kennedy. After his assassination, she switched her allegiance to George McGovern.

Though it was filmed and in the can in 1969, distribution problems held up the release of *Two Mules for Sister Sara,* in which Shirley co-starred with Clint Eastwood, until 1970. Originally, the studio wanted Elizabeth Taylor for the role of the nun-prostitute. When she proved unavailable, they opted for Shirley. "However," said Eastwood, "her casting stretched the imagination quite a bit and required some rewriting." Eastwood thoroughly enjoyed working with Shirley and feels his drunk scene with her is "the best scene I have ever played." The reviews were uniformly fine, and the picture did very well at the box office.

Don't Fall Off the Mountain became a best-seller, topping the hundred-thousand mark in hardcover and paperback. "She writes with grace and wit," said the *New York Times.* Completely self-written, the book charmed and delighted readers everywhere. She bared her life with great candor, showing herself to be alert, sensitive, and endlessly curious. "I wasn't trained to act, and so I thought I couldn't act. I wasn't trained to sing, and so I thought I couldn't sing. I wasn't trained to write, and so I thought I could not write. Then I discovered if one grew enough and knew enough and tried hard enough, one could do those things and be the things one wanted to be. The only thing I was trained to be is a dancer and that's the one thing I'm not," Shirley told the *Saturday Review.*

"Shirley's World," as her ABC-TV series was called, "became for me an experience something akin to what Vietnam must have been to Kennedy, Johnson, and Nixon. You begin by sticking a big toe into the water, and before you know what has happened you are up to your neck in a cesspool."

"Shirley's World" was a disaster from start to finish. It ran seventeen episodes and was canceled. Shirley blamed poor scriptwriting, which made her character, Shirley Logan, world-traveling magazine photographer, an "empty-minded little banana head." She complained the scripts were full of racist clichés about pinching Italians and thieving Arabs.

The show was financed by British media multimillionaire Lord Lew Grade. Part of Shirley's TV deal allowed her to make several films financed by Grade with three-million-dollar budget ceilings. She returned from England and immediately began work on *Desperate Characters.*

Desperate Characters was shot in six weeks in and around New York City. It was brought in complete for three hundred thousand dollars. The whole cast worked for union scale, including Shirley, who got $320 per week, plus a percentage of the profits, if any. "It was an incredible way to work," recalls Shirley. "The only ground rule we had was to stay within the budget. Otherwise we had complete control. When you give an artist that kind of responsibility you're going to get the best out of him."

Shirley remembers they gave her the pay in a small manila envelope and she'd put it in the waist of her slacks. The salary didn't go to an agent or a business manager, and "It was really something I could relate to." And, "Suddenly I became aware of how abstract this whole thing of money is."

Desperate Characters brought a restoration of faith in her abilities as an actress from the critics and the moviegoing public alike. At the 1971 Berlin Film Festival Shirley was a co-winner, with Simone Signoret, of the Silver Bear Award for Best Actress.

Her second film venture for Grade was *The Possession of Joel Delaney,* a contemporary horror tale of the supernatural. It did not fare well with the critics or the public, though in the past few years it has captured an underground cult following. Amid the general rejection of the film, however, Shirley was singled out for many fine reviews of her performance.

What followed was a five-year hiatus from filmmaking. During these years Shirley finished another autobiographical book, *You Can Get There from Here.* She was intensely involved in the presidential campaign of George McGovern, becoming highly vocal and visible on many issues ranging from abortion to the ERA. She took a controversial trip to China, returning with a semidocumentary film that earned her yet another Academy Award nomination, this time as producer and co-director. She also returned to the stage with a revue that broke all existing box-office records at the Palace Theatre in New York and drove the critics wild with praise. Several television specials during these years earned her three Emmy Awards for superb entertainment in that medium.

Shirley and Yves Montand embrace and reminisce about *My Geisha,* in which they co-starred in 1962.

Shirley MacLaine has a special fondness for journalists. She's friends with Pete Hamill of the *New York Daily News,* Martin Tolcher of the *New York Times,* and Marty Nolan of the *Boston Globe.* She traveled in the back of the bus with newspapermen during the McGovern campaign, and she appreciates their problems. Having finished her third book, a novel, she knows what it means to write for a living.

Her drive for achievement is enormous. She told Nancy Collins of the *Washington Post,* "Not trying is always harder than the anticipation of failure if I do try. That's why I started writing.

A serious moment is shared between Shirley and rock superstar Elton John.

It was harder not to write than to write . . . and there's nothing harder than writing."

She's had a relationship with Pete Hamill that's "better and closer" than ever. Until 1976, she had lived with Hamill and his two daughters.

Just as she couldn't settle down in a conventional marriage, she hasn't been able to settle down in a typical relationship with one man. "Settling down doesn't run in our family," she explains.

In 1972, after working for a fruitless year on the McGovern campaign, she endured a crisis that was, she says, worse than her teens. She lost her sense of humor, gained twenty-five pounds, and turned down a lot of film scripts. Then she decided to "go on living positively" by dieting, jogging, exercising, and dancing. She admits she's a "compulsive overachiever" and told reporter Nancy Collins, "when you look back on your life, at your work, your love affairs, your marriages, your pains, your children, your happiness—when you examine all that closely, what you really find out is that the only person you really go to bed with is yourself. The only person you really dress is yourself. The only person you really eat with is yourself." So, in the end, "life must be what you do with yourself."

For years, Shirley MacLaine has been a political activist. Jonas Halperin, now an executive with Warner Bros., points out that "Shirley is not typical Hollywood. When Senator McGovern got murdered in the election, Shirley was at the McGovern headquarters, and she phoned me to say, 'You won't hear from me for about six weeks. I'm renting a car and I'm driving through America. I want to find out why McGovern lost and why so many voted for Nixon.'

"She rented a Chevrolet, drove through the West, into the Southwest, to Los Angeles. She just arrived at places, knocked at doors, and said, 'Hi, I'm traveling around here.' And people said, 'Do I know you?' and she'd say, 'Yeah. I'm Shirley MacLaine.' And they'd invite her in. She'd stay with anybody. When she got back to Los Angeles, she phoned me to report, 'I know why Nixon won, and I'm going to write about it someday.' During her trip, she talked to hundreds of Americans; she stayed with the chief of police of one city; she even went through the jails."

Shirley worked for Bella Abzug in New York and Bella lost. But that didn't depress Shirley. She felt it had been a well-fought fight and they had got some points across. She had worked for the Kennedys (John and Bobby) during the late 50s and early 60s, during Camelot, and she knew Indira Ghandi and Nehru and other heads of state, including Willy Brandt.

She turned down urgings to run for office in

Cigar in mouth, Shirley clowns with old friend and sponsor Lord Lew Grade and his wife, Lady Grade.

New York and in California, confiding to friends, "You can always throw stones better when you are on the outside."

An idealist, she is also pragmatic. At the Democratic convention in Miami, she managed to get the abortion issue put before the convention at 3:00 A.M., so that when the networks televised it, it would not become a big thing. She felt that the abortion issue, at prime time, would have split the Democratic party. "It was a compromise and well thought out," says Jonas Halperin. "Shirley's a smart political animal."

When she's too heavily into politics, she senses it's time to bolster her career. When she returned from her trip to China, which resulted in a TV documentary, she decided to return to the stage after twenty years. She confided to Jonas Halperin, "We've done the political thing, and now a little tits and ass won't hurt. We're going through so much shit in the world, a little laughter won't hurt now. I'd like to go out and really have the audience jump and laugh and carry on and learn a little more about me!"

Halperin says, "Shirley has orchestrated her life so as to touch everything. To enjoy the touch of everything is the most important thing to her. She wants to be involved in as much as possible. But she doesn't feel that just because you're very serious about political convictions you can't earn a living and entertain."

Her political activities have drawn criticism, of course. Her own father, a Nixon partisan, once asked her, "Why don't you go back to doing what you do best and stop all the preaching around?" A trade-paper columnist used to call her a dingbat for speaking out in public.

Her friends insist that she isn't upset by negative publicity but that she is stung by criticism of her political activities, especially when the criticism is unfair, like the charge that she did a propaganda film for Mainland China.

In her book *You Can Get There from Here,* Shirley MacLaine recalls that the old movie moguls were "hard-fisted authoritarians" who created "linked dictatorships" to control creative people. "We [actors] were supposed to be the children; mad, tempestuous, brilliant, talented, not terribly smart children." The moguls "led, guided, manipulated, bought, sold, packaged, coddled, and tolerated" the actors. Therefore, she says, she's not surprised when some stars become dictators too.

But career power and wealth have never been her goals. "I don't have a car," she told Merv Griffin. "I don't have a house. I have a fur coat for posing for an ad. I've got some money someplace, but I never see it."

She's aware, of course, that she has "tremendous earning power," but she tries to simplify her life by having few material possessions. "I have a small apartment, designed for me to be able to leave it. I have my home in the air when I'm in a plane, and a hotel room when I'm traveling. I travel with only one bag."

Her New York duplex apartment has one bedroom upstairs, a bedroom downstairs, a den, a living room, a small dining room, and a galley kitchen with a tiny table. She doesn't care for jewelry (she's been robbed many times) and there are only four or five outfits in her wardrobe closet. An airline credit card and a phone credit card mean the most; they get her in touch with people. She got rid of her big house in Encino, California, and has a small place on the beach at Malibu.

She seems to be embarrassed by displays of

Shirley MacLaine, about 1978.

Discussing Far Eastern matters comes easily to Shirley. Here she is speaking with Dewi Sukarno, wife of the president of Indonesia.

wealth; she hates traveling by chauffeured limousine. When she arrived in Paris, the promoters of the Olympia Theatre had a chauffeured Rolls-Royce waiting for her and a Volkswagen for her luggage. But she insisted on traveling in the Volks with her secretary and let her agent ride in the Rolls. Later she drove through Europe in the Volks.

Her interests are not those of stereotypical American women. She doesn't bother with small talk about food, houses, fashions. At a gathering, within fifteen minutes, the aware people start moving toward MacLaine because she's talking about vital subjects. She's talking about China, India, Africa, politics. She'll say, "Did you hear what the ambassador said about so-an-so?"

Not only is she a great talker, but she's a great listener, too. Halperin says, "She absorbs, absorbs, remembers. When you say to her, 'I'll see you at 4:25 three weeks from now at the corner,' she'll phone and say, 'Hey, where were you at 4:25 at the corner?' She has total recall. She'll tell you, for instance, 'Didn't you tell me four years ago that you saw that movie and didn't like it?' "

She told Nancy Collins of the *Washington Post,* "Life is a feast to me; sometimes I'm hungry and sometimes I'm not. I do know women who have four lovers at once, and I'm amazed. If I had all that going on, I wouldn't be able to figure out when to jog and when to make love."

Her relationship with her brother, Warren, is often gossiped about. She explains that the relationship is misunderstood because they're not together much. Shirley lives in New York and he in California, in two rooms in the Beverly Wilshire Hotel, even though he owns a house that's been renovated into a palace.

When the president's mother, Miss Lillian, visited Shirley in Malibu, she said she wanted to meet Warren. So Warren came over to Shirley's, and after Miss Lillian went to bed, he stayed to chat with his sister till 8:00 A.M. He is politically aware but not the flamboyant activist his older sister is.

She's gone through the mill. She knows what's it's all about. She's cynical. She wants people to be straight with her; she respects the truth. She'll tell friends, "Don't con me! Don't tell me I'm great! Don't kiss my ass!" In 1977, when trade-paper reviews on *The Turning Point* came out, her friend Jonas Halperin said, "The trade reviews are really terrific!" and she snapped, "Yes, so what? The trade reviewers were good on *Goldfarb* and on *My Geisha,* which were disasters. So, wait till *Turning Point* gets to the public!"

She won her fourth Oscar nomination for *The Turning Point,* and the film had special meaning for her. She explained to Merv Griffin on his talk show, "When we first read the script, I said, 'What is this?' She is pregnant and has to make a choice between having a baby and having a career. Why can't she have both? *I* did it! A lot of women I know did it! But . . . the action takes place 20 years ago when it was not that easy to get an abortion. In fact, it was impossible. And women thought they only had that choice.

"My character [in the movie] had the feeling her frustrations were real. Her dreams were thwarted. That's probably the most painful thing anyone can live with: not having ever found out whether they could or couldn't be good enough at what they wanted to express."

And she adds, "The worst is not to know who you are. You can go through a lot of love affairs, a lot of marriages, a lot of children, a lot of success. If you don't know that, you don't know anything."

No, she is not fulfilled, she assured Griffin. "I have so much more to do and so much more to find out and so much more to try! The thing I would really hate is to be young again. The confusion . . . that lack of definition . . . that wondering!"

The Films of Shirley MacLaine

Jerry Mathers shows his mother, Shirley MacLaine, the body he has discovered while playing in the woods.

The Trouble With Harry

Paramount / 1955

CREDITS:

Producer-director, Alfred Hitchcock; based on the novel by John Trevor Story; screenplay, John Michael Hayes; music, Bernard Herrmann; song, Mack David, Raymond Scott; art direction, Hal Pereira, John Goodman; special effects, John P. Fulton; cinematographer, Robert Burks; editor, Alma Macrorie. Running time: 99 minutes. Technicolor.

CAST:

Edmund Gwenn *(Captain Albert Wiles)*; John Forsythe *(Sam Marlowe)*; Shirley MacLaine

Shirley MacLaine, as she first appears in *The Trouble with Harry*.

Confused by the presence of Harry, in the tub, are Jerry Mathers, Shirley MacLaine, and Sheriff Royal Dano.

(Jennifer Rogers); Mildred Natwick *(Miss Gravely)*; Jerry Mathers *(Tony Rogers)*; Mildred Dunnock *(Mrs. Wiggs)*; Royal Dano *(Alfred Wiggs)*; Parker Fennelly *(millionaire)*; Barry Macollum *(tramp)*; Dwight Marfield *(Dr. Greenbow)*; Leslie Woolf *(art critic)*; Philip Truex *(Harry Worp)*; Ernest Curt Bach *(chauffeur)*.

SYNOPSIS:

Young Tony Rogers (Jerry Mathers) discovers a body in the woods. He quickly brings his mother, Jennifer (Shirley MacLaine), to see the body. Jennifer immediately recognizes the body as that of her former husband, Harry. She feels responsible for his death, having bashed him with a whiskey bottle. Captain Wiles (Edmund Gwenn) feels he may have done Harry in with a stray shot from his rifle, while hunting rabbits in the vicinity. Miss Gravely (Mildred Natwick), an old maid, is also sure that in some way she's to blame for Harry's demise.

Abstract painter Sam Marlowe (John Forsythe), who, like the rest, harbored no great love for Harry, also finds himself involved in burying

Four possible murder suspects: Edmund Gwenn, Shirley MacLaine, John Forsythe, and Mildred Natwick.

Love interest develops between abstract painter Forsythe and youthful widow MacLaine.

and reburying Harry's body as all those "responsible" try to cover up.

But Harry won't stay put for long, finally reappearing in a bathtub. At last it is discovered that Harry died of natural causes and all are "exonerated." In the meantime, Jennifer and Sam have kindled a romance, and Captain Wiles has found love with Miss Gravely.

REVIEWS:

There's an especially disarming screwball blandness about the manner of Miss MacLaine.

New York Times

[She] shows a flair for comedy in an apparently guileless straight faced style that is thoroughly her own.

Christian Science Monitor

Miss MacLaine impressed despite the handicap of some highschool, amateur mannerisms, which manage to get by here but will need correction for the future.

Variety

NOTES:

In *The Trouble with Harry,* director Hitchcock sought to make the backgrounds as much a part of the story as the characters and the plot. He wished to achieve a dramatic backdrop against

Hitchcock, greeting his newest discovery as she arrives on the set, later called her "a great dramatic actress."

which the action would take place—the lives of simple and attractive people in a framework of awesome beauty.

His searching party found the ideal spot in Vermont, where vast mountainsides are covered with maples and oaks. The headquarters for production activity was Stowe. From Stowe, Hitchcock, his cast, and his crew radiated out to a beautiful little village on the crest of a mountain, Craftsbury Common; to East Craftsbury, a few miles away; to Morrisville, where the gymnasium of the local American Legion was rigged up as a sound stage for interior shooting; and to the Sugarbush area, where, amid the lush maple trees, the scenes of interment and disinterment were enacted.

Hitchcock remarks today that *The Trouble with Harry* is "one of my favorite pictures" and "the only losing picture I've had since 1952." Hitch supposes the film didn't do well at the box office because it had "no well-known stars on which it could be sold."

Hitchcock told author Charles Higham, in his book *The Celluloid Muse,* "I found the story in a small English novel and changed the setting to Vermont in autumn, because I wanted to counterpoint its macabre elements with beautifully colored scenery. Shirley MacLaine, whose first film this was, had been understudying in the musical *Pajama Game*. Hal Wallis had her under contract and I saw a test of her he'd made."

Bumbling Jerry Lewis destroys a water cooler as a distressed Shirley MacLaine and a young bystander look on.

Artists and Models

Paramount / 1955

CREDITS:

Producer, Hal Wallis; associate producer, Paul Nathan; director, Frank Tashlin; based on the story "Rock-a-Bye Baby," by Michael Davidson and Norman Lessine; adaptation, Don McGuire; screenplay, Frank Tashlin, Hal Kanter, Herbert Baker; art direction, Hal Pereira and Tambi Larsen; music director, Walter Scharf; songs, Harry Warren, Jack Brooks; cinematographer, Daniel L. Fapp; editor, Warren Low. Running time: 109 minutes. Color. VistaVision.

CAST:

Dean Martin (*Rick Todd*); Jerry Lewis (*Eugene Fullstack*); Shirley MacLaine (*Bessie Sparrowbush*); Dorothy Malone (*Abigail Parker*); Eddie Mayehoff (*Mr. Murdock*); Eva Gabor (*Sonia*); Anita Ekberg (*Anita*); George Winslow (*Richard Stilton*); Jack Elam (*Ivan*); Herbert Rudley (*Secret Service Chief Samuels*); Richard Shannon (*Secret Service Agent Rogers*); Richard Webb (*Secret Service Agent Peters*); Alan Lee (*Otto*); Kathleen Freeman (*Mrs. Muldoon*); Art Baker (*himself*); Emory Parnell (*Kelly*); Carleton Young (*Colonel Drury*); Nick Castle (*specialty dancer*).

SYNOPSIS:

Rick Todd (Dean Martin) is a frustrated artist living in Greenwich Village. Unable to make a sufficient living, he enters into a deal with Mr. Murdock (Eddie Mayehoff), a comic-book publisher, to draw strips, providing he can come up with wild, original ideas. Rick soon becomes partners with Eugene Fullstack (Jerry Lewis), who provides him with ideas and inspirations via his woolly nightmare ravings. Love interests are

Secretary Shirley turns a pretty leg as comic artist Dean Martin looks on grumpily.

provided by Abigail Parker (Dorothy Malone) and Bessie Sparrowbush (Shirley MacLaine), who live next door.

The boys' violent ideas for comics come under attack from pressure groups. In a hilarious sequence, Eugene goes on a live TV talk show before a panel, to debate the effects of comics on kids.

As Rick woos Abigail, Bessie goes after Eugene, agreeing to pose for him as the weird Bat Lady, for a special strip he is working on. When Bessie's advances fail to spark a marriage proposal from nutty Eugene, ingenious Bessie sits on the frantic Eugene until he complies.

REVIEW:

Miss MacLaine has the makings of a lively comedienne, as she shows in one comic dance

The weird Bat Lady has been chasing Jerry Lewis without luck so far. Here, she takes a breather.

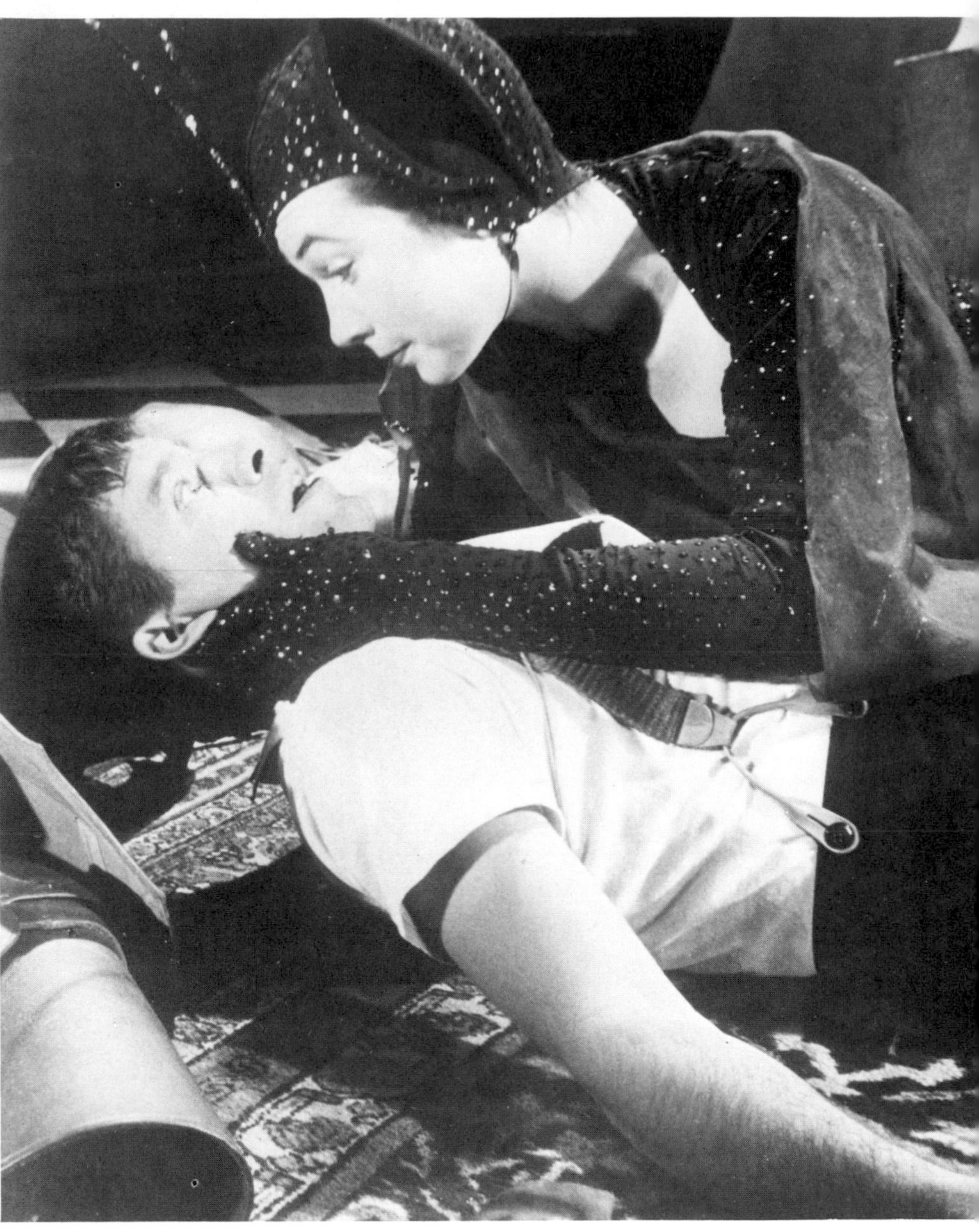

Shirley, as the exotic Bat Lady, attempts to seduce a scared Jerry Lewis.

with Jerry and in a couple of passing scenes. But the script does not give her material. . . . Maybe next time, Hal Wallis, the film's producer, will let Jerry and Miss MacLaine go it together without Dean or anyone to get in their way.

New York Times

NOTES:

This film introduced Shirley to Dean Martin, who was to become her lifelong friend. They went on to make five films together, making Dean the leading man she has appeared with most. Their friendship deepened when they worked together in 1958 in Indiana on the film *Some Came Running*. It was there Shirley was baptized an official member of Sinatra's newly formed Clan, AKA the Rat Pack. Shirley was the only female and was quickly made the mascot.

Artists and Models marked the debut of Shirley's singing voice on film, and if anything was quickly apparent, it was that she'd received no coaching from Dean Martin. As Dean begins to croon in one scene, Shirley follows on the refrain, in tones unmistakably all her own.

Cantinflas and Shirley are eyed warily on the boat deck by police inspector Robert Newton.

Around the World in 80 Days

United Artists / 1956

CREDITS:

Producer, Mike Todd; director, Michael Anderson; screenplay, James Poe, John Farrow, S. J. Perelman; based on the novel by Jules Verne; music, Victor Young; associate producer, William Cameron Menzies; second-unit director, Kevin O'Donovan McClory; cinematographer, Lionel Lindon; editors, Paul Weatherwax, Gene Ruggiero; art director, James Sullivan; set decorator, Ross Dowd; costume designer, Miles White; choreographer, Paul Godkin; sound, Joseph Kane; special effects, Lee Zavitz; makcup, Gustav Norin; hair stylist, Edith Keon; sound effects, Ted Bellinger. Running time: 178 minutes. Technicolor. (Todd-AO.)

CAST:

David Niven *(Phineas Fogg)*; Cantinflas *(Passepartout)*; Shirley MacLaine *(Princess Aouda)*; Robert Newton *(Inspector Fix)*; Joe E. Brown *(station master)*; Martine Carol *(tourist)*; John

A much-darkened Shirley portraying the Indian Princess Aouda.

Carradine (*Colonel Proctor Stamp*); Charles Coburn (*clerk*); Ronald Colman (*railway official*); Melville Cooper (*steward*); Noël Coward (*Hesketh-Baggott*); Finlay Currie (*whist partner*); Reginald Denny (*police chief*); Andy Devine (*first mate*); Marlene Dietrich (*hostess*); Luis Miguel Dominguin (*bullfighter*); Fernandel (*coachman*); John Gielgud (*Foster*); Hermione Gingold (*lady*); Jose Greco (*dancer*); Cedric Hardwicke (*Sir Francis Gromarty*); Trevor Howard (*Fallentin*); Glynis Johns (*companion*); Buster Keaton (*conductor*); Evelyn Keyes (*flirt*); Beatrice Lillie (*revivalist*); Peter Lorre (*steward*); Edmund Lowe (*engineer*); Victor McLaglen (*helmsman*); A. E. Mathews (*club member*); Mike Mazurki (*character*); John Mills (*cabby*); Alan Mowbray (*consul*); Robert Morley (*Ralph*); Edward R. Murrow (*narrator*); Jack Oakie (*captain*); George Raft (*bouncer*); Gilbert Roland (*Achmed Abdullah*); Cesar Romero (*henchman*); Frank Sinatra (*piano player*); Red Skelton (*drunk*); Ava Gardner (*spectator*); Basil Sydney (*club member*); Ronald Squire (*club member*); Harcourt Williams (*aged steward*).

SYNOPSIS:

In 1872, at the Victorian Reform Club in London, member Phineas Fogg (David Niven) boasts he can circle the globe in eighty days. His fellow club members wager him twenty thousand

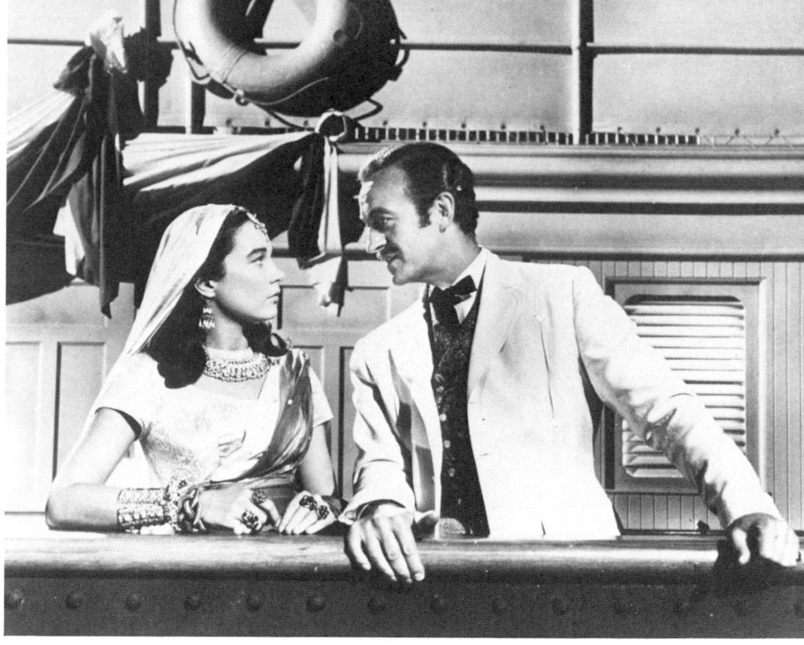

The romance of MacLaine and Niven begins aboard ship as they leave Calcutta and head for Hong Kong.

pounds Sterling that he is wrong. He accepts their wager, and with his faithful valet, Passepartout (Cantinflas), in tow, he sets out for Paris.

Along thc way, an avalanchc stops their train. Fogg buys a balloon and, heading south, is blown off-course to Spain. Passepartout's gymnastics in a bullring impress an Arabian sheik, who provides transport to Marseille, where Fogg and valet catch a steamer to India. On their trail is Inspector Fix, who is convinced that Fogg is responsible for robbing the Bank of England.

In India, Fogg and Passepartout rescue Princess Aouda (Shirley MacLaine) from being burned alive in a suttee ceremony, and she

Stopping during their train ride across the American West are Shirley, David Niven, Cantinflas, and Buster Keaton.

quickly joins them on their journey. Fogg is arrested in Calcutta by cronies of Fix and jumps bail, heading for Hong Kong. Fix has Passepartout shanghaied to Japan, where Fogg comes via Chinese junk and rescues him.

They sail for San Francisco, from where they head east toward New York. Captured by Indians, Passepartout is once more rescued by Fogg, but valued time is lost. Late for the New York boat to Liverpool, Fogg bribes a schooner captain headed for South America to change course for England.

In Liverpool, Fogg, is arrested by Fix. Hours later, cleared of the charge of bank robbery, Fogg is released. In London, Fogg and party arrive at the club, but they are five minutes too late. Aouda and Fogg decide to marry, and Passepartout is sent to make the wedding arrangements. Passepartout discovers that they have gained a day's time crossing East to West

Entering a Japanese theater in Tokyo, Niven and MacLaine are shocked to find missing manservant Cantinflas working as an acrobat.

Aboard the train heading west are poker players Robert Newton, Shirley, Cantinflas, and David Niven.

and swiftly informs all. They rush to the club just in time to claim the prize in triumph.

REVIEWS:

Outside of Cantinflas and David Niven, who is excellent as the punctual Phineas Fogg, there are the late Robert Newton as Fix, the detective; Shirley MacLaine as Princess Aouda, and an assortment of bit players ranging from Noël Coward to Jack Oakie. . . . All and sundry play their roles honorably.

New York Times

Big, splashy. The actors are all fine, and the scenic effects are tremendous!

New Yorker

Titanic, titillating, and thrilling . . . it's a pip!

New York Mirror

A marvelous movie . . . "Supermagnagorgeous." Prodigious array of wonder, splendor, sights and sounds.

Christian Science Monitor

Ranks among the greatest motion pictures . . . pure joy all the way.

Film Daily

The biggest and most successful movies ordinarily create little stir on Broadway. But Mike Todd's fantastic "what-is-it" . . . so new that nobody could describe it . . . does just that!

Newsweek

The human race has never before seen entertainment such as this. Greatest show now on earth!

National Board of Review

NOTES:

When Mike Todd offered Shirley the chance to play a "campy Hindu princess" in a film that would do part of its shooting in Japan, Shirley leaped at the chance, knowing she'd get to spend cherished time with her husband, Steve Parker, who had decided to live in Japan.

The filming of *Around the World in 80*

Days was the largest logistical undertaking ever made by a film company.

Master showman-producer Mike Todd employed 68,894 people in thirteen countries. Four million air miles were flown; 680,000 feet of film was exposed; 74,685 costumes were required by wardrobe to dress, in period, 6,400 Spaniards, 2,672 Japanese, 3,600 Muslims, 1,927 Arabs, 1,688 American Indians, 1,553 Englishmen, and 1,664 Frenchmen. It was the biggest job ever given the Western Costume Company of Hollywood, the largest in America, in its forty-year history.

Seventy make-up artists were employed gluing beards on 15,612 chins.

Shooting was done in 112 natural settings, on 140 specially constructed sets, in 32 foreign locations, and in 11 major studios. It had the most camera setups ever used: 2,000. The film was edited down to 22,000 feet, approximately two hours and forty minutes on the screen.

More than 100,000 hot meals were served the cast and crew during filming.

It employed the most major stars to appear in a film together, 47. In its initial release, *Around the World in 80 Days* grossed better than $21,000,000 and played 102 weeks straight on Broadway in New York City.

The ebullient trio, Cantinflas, Niven, and MacLaine, head for the club in London, assured they have won their original wager.

Glenn Ford, as a sheepherder, eventually wins the hand of the cattle baron's daughter, played by Shirley.

The Sheepman

Metro-Goldwyn-Mayer / 1958

CREDITS:

Producer, Edmund Grainger; director, George Marshall; based on a story by James Edward Grant; adaptation, William Roberts; screenplay, William Bowers Grant; art direction, William A. Horning, Malcolm Brown; music, Jeff Alexander; assistant director, Al Jennings; cinematographer, Robert Bronner; editor, Ralph E. Winters. Running time: 85 minutes. Metrocolor.

CAST:

Glenn Ford *(Jason Sweet)*; Shirley MacLaine *(Dell Payton)*; Leslie Nielsen *(Johnny Bledsoe, alias Colonel Stephen Bedford)*; Mickey Shaughnessy *(Jumbo McCall)*; Edgar Buchanan *(Milt Masters)*; Wilis Bouchey *(Mr. Payton)*; Pernell Roberts *(Choctaw)*; Slim Pickens *(marshal)*; Buzz Henry *(Red)*; Pedro Gonzales Gonzales *(Angelo)*.

SYNOPSIS:

In 1880, onto the open rangelands of Powder Valley rides Jason Sweet, an easygoing sheepman bringing his herd into cattle country. His entry is opposed by the whole town, from local gunslinger Jumbo McCall to pretty Dell Payton, fiancée of local cattle baron Colonel Stephen

Mickey Shaughnessy and a henchman ask Glenn Ford to visit their boss, Leslie Nielsen. Shirley watches Ford's reaction.

Sheepherder Glenn Ford meets bad-guy cattleman Leslie Nielsen, as Shirley watches.

Shirley portrays the lovely Dell Payton in her first Western.

Bedford—all of whom fear that the stranger's sheep will overgraze the land, leaving nothing for the beef cattle.

When Bedford's hired gunslingers raid Jason's camp and kill several of his men, the sheepman retaliates by exposing Bedford's shady past as an outlaw named Johnny Bledsoe. Sweet then gains the admiration of the townfolk—and the heart of Dell Payton—by bravely winning a three-to-one gun battle.

REVIEWS:

Her hair delicately crimson in Metrocolor, [she] flits with an insouciant air, as the rancher's daughter. Miss MacLaine's charm is as much as anything else responsible for the film's genial irresistibility. She has an abrupt and cackling laugh that springs alive from her throat and a little girl's forthrightness that fits the role like a wedding dress.

New York Herald Tribune

Miss MacLaine is a most unlikely heroine in a sloppy felt hat and jeans . . . a perfect comedy foil for Ford.

Variety

Likewise amusing is loose-jointed Shirley MacLaine. . . . Her blissful nonchalance in times of crisis and her casualness with frivolous remarks help to preserve the tone of mockery that is the nicest thing about this film.

New York Times

An anxious Shirley tries to dissuade Glenn Ford from stepping out into a gunfight.

If you want proof that [director] Marshall knows his trade, notice how much nicer Shirley MacLaine is here than she was in *The Trouble with Harry,* and how much better an actress she is here than in *Hot Spell.*

Films in Review

NOTES:

The critics heartily enjoyed MacLaine's performance, and the years since have shown *The Sheepman* to be one of the better adult Westerns to come out of Hollywood in the 1950s.

Veteran character actor and co-star Edgar Buchanan recalls working on *The Sheepman:* "That was a good picture. We had a ball. I thought Shirley MacLaine was just great. George Marshall is the greatest comedy director in pictures, has been for half a century."

As the *New York Times* had said, *The Sheepman* "treats the standard rivalry [between cattlemen and sheepmen] with humor and a certain amount of spoof."

Shirley MacLaine gets the drop on bad guy Mickey Shaughnessy as he was on the way to ambush Glenn Ford.

Shirley Booth comforts her daughter, Shirley MacLaine, who has just been humiliated by her father for necking with her boyfriend.

Hot Spell

Paramount / 1958

CREDITS:

Producer, Hal B. Wallis; associate producer, Paul Nathan; director, Daniel Mann; based on the play *Next of Kin,* by Lonnie Coleman; screenplay, James Poe; music, Alex North; art direction, Hal Pereira, Tambi Larsen; cinematographer, Loyal Griggs; editor, Warren Low; special effects, John P. Fulton. Running Time: 86 minutes. VistaVision. Black and white.

CAST:

Shirley Booth *(Alma Duval)*; Anthony Quinn *(Jack Duval)*; Shirley MacLaine *(Virginia Duval)*; Earl Holliman *(Buddy Duval)*; Eileen Heckart *(fan)*; Clint Kimbrough *(Billy Duval)*; Warren Stevens *(Wyatt)*; Jody Lawrence *(Dora May)*; Harlan Warde *(Harry)*; Valerie Allen *(Ruby)*; Stafford Repp *(baggage man)*; Irene Tedrow *(Essie Mae)*; Bill Walker *(attendant)*; Louise Franklin *(colored woman)*; Anthony Jochim *(preacher)*; Johnny Lee *(colored man)*; Elsie Waller *(librarian)*; Len Hendry, John Indrisano *(pool players)*; Watson H. Downs *(funeral-car driver)*; William Duray *(conductor)*.

SYNOPSIS:

While New Orleans is being visited by a hot spell, middle-aged Alma Duval is dreaming of a happier time in the past, as she prepares a surprise birthday party for her husband, Jack. Alma hopes the party, complete with presents she has bought for her three grown children to give to their father, will bring him back to her. The party turns into a vivid psychological brawl as Jack (Anthony Quinn) rips into his son for desiring a business of his own, financed by a loan from his father, which Jack is unwilling to negotiate.

Rejected and furious, Buddy (Earl Holliman), runs off into the night to get drunk. He is soon followed by his sensitive, quiet younger brother, Billy.

As Jack leaves the house he finds his daughter, Virginia (Shirley MacLaine), necking with her boyfriend, Wyatt (Warren Stevens), on the porch. Jack overwhelms and embarrasses both by questioning their conduct, after which he asks Wyatt his intentions.

Shirley Booth talks to daughter Shirley MacLaine of happier times, as she decorates a birthday cake for her husband.

Jack finds Billy (Clint Kimbrough) outside and takes him to the local pool hall to instruct him on the finer points of the game and for an overdue father-son talk. Their conversation quickly deteriorates as Jack sees he cannot make the boy understand his frustrations as a husband and father. Realizing they are more strangers than father and son, Jack tells Billy he has a "business" appointment to keep, then leaves. Following his father, Billy sees him rendezvous

Photo of a movie poster for *Hot Spell.*

Warren Stevens, whom Shirley has fallen for, quietly tells her of his intention to marry a wealthy woman.

Earl Holliman talks to his sister, Shirley MacLaine, and his mother, Shirley Booth, of the estrangement he feels from his father.

Earl Holliman tries to comfort his mother, Shirley Booth, as his brother, Clint Kimbrough, and sister, Shirley MacLaine, watch and they all await the arrival of Anthony Quinn's body at the train station.

and drive off with Ruby (Valerie Allen). Billy now sees the result of his father's frustrations and the sad realization opens a new door toward his growth into a man.

REVIEWS:

The only thing worth noting . . . is the change in appearance and acting style, of Shirley MacLaine. A change from what she was in *The Trouble with Harry* that is, I'm delighted to say, for the better.

Films in Review

Also superior is Shirley MacLaine.

New York Times

Others do well despite insufficiently conceived roles.

Variety

Superb acting and fine direction.

New York Herald Tribune

NOTES:

Hot Spell was based on the play *Next of Kin,* by Lonnie Coleman, which did not receive a Broadway production.

Based on the potential she showed as a dramatic actress while performing onstage in *The Sleeping Prince,* Hal Wallis offered Shirley the role of Ginny in *Hot Spell.* It meant co-starring status after two films in which she'd received star billing, but Shirley grabbed it, knowing that it would boost her stock as a serious dramatic actress after her appearing in lighter vehicles.

She learned a great deal about acting from the masterful Shirley Booth and began taking her craft more seriously after this role.

Often, after emotionally trying scenes Shirley would go into fits of screaming, which were tactfully ignored by actors and stagehands, to work off the intense turmoil she had been experiencing.

A very youthful Tony Perkins guides a demure Shirley across the dance floor on their first date.

The Matchmaker

Paramount / 1958

CREDITS:

Producer, Don Hartman; director, Joseph Anthony; based on the play by Thornton Wilder; screenplay, John Michael Hayes; art direction, Hal Pereira, Roland Anderson; music, Adolph Deutsch; cinematographer, Charles Lang; editor, Howard Smith. Running time: 101 minutes. VistaVision. Black and white.

CAST:

Shirley Booth *(Dolly Levi)*; Anthony Perkins *(Cornelius)*; Shirley MacLaine *(Irene Molloy)*; Paul Ford *(Horace Vandergelder)*; Robert Morse *(Barnaby Tucker)*; Perry Wilson *(Minnie Fay)*; Wallace Ford *(Malachi Stack)*; Russell Collins *(Joe Scanlon)*; Rex Evans *(August)*; Gavin Gordon *(Rudolph)*; Torben Meyer *(maitre d')*.

SYNOPSIS:

In 1884, Yonkers matchmaker Dolly Levi leads her client Horace Vandergelder to New York City, ostensibly to introduce him to young milliner Irene Molloy, but actually Dolly has plans to snare the wealthy merchant for herself. Vandergelder's two poor clerks, Cornelius and Barnaby, left behind to watch the store, also decide to go to New York City, each determined to have the "dangerous adventure" of kissing a pretty girl.

Fatefully they meet Irene and her girlfriend Minnie Fay and take them to dine at one of Manhattan's classiest restaurants. The problem of funds with which to pay the check is solved when Cornelius recovers Vandergelder's lost wallet, as he happens to be dining in the next room with Dolly.

Wealthy merchant Paul Ford pours champagne for the object of his desire, the lovely Shirley MacLaine, as Perry Wilson blinks.

When Vandergelder discovers the double deception, both clerks are fired and Dolly finds herself in danger of losing her fee and her prospective husband. Undaunted, Dolly sets up Cornelius in a rival store across the street from Vandergelder. Her superb machinations prove too much for the merchant Vandergelder—he quickly agrees to take on young Cornelius as his parner and Dolly as his wife.

REVIEWS:

Shirley MacLaine is a great asset. . . . Her face,

Fearing their boss will discover they are not at work but dining in the same restaurant as he is, Tony Perkins and Bobby Morse try to hide as Shirley frantically helps them.

Anthony Perkins joyfully renews his friendship with his former boss, Paul Ford, as (left to right) Wallace Ford, Robert Morse, Shirley MacLaine, Perry Wilson, and Shirley Booth happily approve.

of itself, is enough to ensure success as a comedienne. . . . If in the next few years she learns as much as she has in the last two or three, she should be one of the most popular actresses of the next decade.

Films in Review

Shirley MacLaine seems to have trouble trying to make something amusing of her role.

New York Herald Tribune

Anthony Perkins, Paul Ford, and Shirley MacLaine provide some comedy, too.

Saturday Review

Miss MacLaine is pert and lovely.

Variety

. . . And Shirley MacLaine is properly sweet, demure and confused.

New York Times

NOTES:

The play on which the film was based was first presented in 1938 as *The Merchant of Yonkers.* The stage version of this film opened at the Royale Theatre on December 5, 1955. Ruth Gordon, Arthur Hill, Eileen Herlie, and Loring Smith created the roles played respectively by Booth, Perkins, MacLaine, and Paul Ford. Robert Morse is repeating his original role. The Theatre Guild and David Merrick produced and Tyrone Guthrie directed.

Perry Wilson, incidentally, is the wife of director Joseph Anthony.

Before he returns home from the army, Frank Sinatra picks up a dim-witted whore, Shirley MacLaine, in a saloon.

Some Came Running

Metro-Goldwyn-Mayer / 1958

CREDITS:

Producer, Sol C. Siegel; director, Vincente Minnelli; based on the novel by James Jones; screenplay, John Patrick, Arthur Sheekman; music, Elmer Bernstein; song, James Van Heusen, Sammy Cahn; art direction, William A. Horning, Urie McCleary; set decoration, Henry Grace, Robert Priestley; costumes, Walter Plunkett; makcup, William Tuttle; assistant director, William McGarry; cinematographer, William H. Daniels; editor, Adrienne Fazan. Running time: 127 minutes. MetroColor. Cinemascope.

CAST:

Frank Sinatra *(Dave Hirsh)*; Dean Martin *(Bama Dillert)*; Shirley MacLaine *(Ginny Moorhead)*; Martha Hyer *(Gwen French)*; Arthur Kennedy *(Frank Hirsh)*; Nancy Gates *(Edith Barclay)*; Leora Dana *(Agnes Hirsh)*; Betty Lou Keim *(Dawn Hirsh)*; Carmen Phillips *(Rosalie)*; Steven Peck *(Raymond Lanchak)*; Connie Gilchrist *(Jane Barclay)*; John Brennan *(Wally Dennis)*; Larry Gates *(Professor Robert Haven French)*; Ned Wever *(Smitty)*; Denny Miller *(Dewey Cole)*; Don Haggerty *(Ted Harperspoon)*; William Shallert *(Al)*; Geraldine Wall *(Mrs. Stevens)*; Janelle Richards *(Virginia Stevens)*; George E. Stone *(Slim)*; Anthony Jochim *(Judge Baskin)*; Marion Ross *(Sister Mary Joseph)*; Ric Roman *(Joe)*; Roy Engel *(sheriff)*; Elmer Petersen *(radio announcer)*.

SYNOPSIS:

Discharged from the army, Dave Hirsh returns to his small hometown in Indiana with nothing

"My favorite role," said MacLaine of her portrayal of Ginny Moorhead, for which she received her first Academy Award nomination for Best Actress.

Frank Sinatra and Shirley MacLaine have one of their many arguments as solitaire-playing Dean Martin and his girl, Carmen Phillips, stay cool.

Frank Sinatra, an aspiring writer, berates Shirley for autographing his magazine article for her friends at work.

more than an unpublished manuscript and a happy-go-lucky whore named Ginny, who has mistaken his drunken overtures for genuine affection. Though he brushes her off when sober, she doggedly remains, hoping he'll change his mind.

Dave's older brother, Frank (Arthur Kennedy), is a wealthy local businessman who resents Dave's relationship with Ginny, although Frank is having an affair with his secretary. Dave in turn hates Frank for shipping him off to an orphanage when they were younger.

A local college instructor, Gwen French (Martha Hyer), takes an interest in Dave and his writing. Bama Dillert (Dean Martin) and Dave

Shirley and Frank try to talk his drunken niece, played by Betty Lou Keim, into going back home to her parents.

The pathetic, but touching scene between two losers, sloppy Shirley and frigid Martha Hyer.

Knowing very well who and what she is, Frank asks Shirley to marry him.

The famous death scene, wherein Shirley steps in front of Frank Sinatra and is killed by the bullet meant for him.

Shirley poses with a puppy during a break in the shooting.

become drinking and gambling partners, even though Bama berates Dave over his relationship with Ginny. Although enamored of Gwen, Dave keeps Ginny available and waiting while he pursues the icy college instructor. Try as he might, Dave cannot melt the barriers between himself and Gwen, and he finally gives up when she refuses to marry him.

Disappointed and disillusioned, Dave grabs Ginny and Bama, and they take off across the state on a sad binge. In Terre Haute, the trio encounter Frank's teenaged daughter, Dawn, who has run away from home with her boyfriend after discovering the affair her father has carried on with his secretary. Dave returns Dawn to her parents, denounces them for their moral hypocrisy, and leaves. He then stuns Bama by announcing his intention to marry Ginny.

Shortly after their marriage, Ginny's jealous former boyfriend, Raymond Lanchak (Steven Peck), attempts to murder Dave. Ginny is wounded fatally as she attempts to shield Dave from her ex-boyfriend's lethal gunfire. In the middle of a local carnival she dies in the arms of Dave.

REVIEWS:

It is Shirley MacLaine, with a moving portrayal of the giddy and warm-hearted tart that might well win an Academy Award.

Cosmopolitan

Compensation for the film's inadequacies is to be found in Shirley MacLaine's portrait of an over-ripe piece of goods who blows into town from Chicago. She is the brightest feature.

Newsweek

But the surprise hit is Shirley MacLaine's touching, unforgettable portrait of the crude, pathetic little floozy who falls in love with Frank.

Los Angeles Mirror-News

Brilliant overacting by Shirley MacLaine.

Time

Miss MacLaine portrays a young woman out on

While waiting for a camera setup, Frank helps Shirley adjust a bracelet clasp.

Shirley relaxes with a cigarette after a long day of filming.

On the set, Shirley listens to director Vincente Minnelli make suggestions for an upcoming scene.

her own in the world, who admits she doesn't understand many things, but knows, nevertheless, that she is in love with Sinatra. Her elfin quality shines through the veneer and makes her characterization sympathetic.

Motion Picture Herald

NOTES:

Shirley received her first Academy Award nomination for Best Actress in 1958 for her work in this film. The role of Ginny Moorhead is the one she has always considered her favorite.

Shirley recalled in her autobiography, *Don't Fall Off the Mountain,* "It was on location for *Some Came Running,* in Madison, Indiana, that my relationship with the so-called clan started. *Clan* was coined by a national-magazine reporter assigned to write a story on the production of the picture and the characters involved. No one would see him, so he called us the clan."

The people of Madison kept a twenty-four-hour vigil around the house where the cast had their quarters, hoping to get a glimpse of Frank or Dean or Shirley. Shirley was the only woman allowed in their house. "I spent a lot of time there, tidying up for them, arranging flowers and putting candy on the tables. All they did was play gin, but they were more fun to be around than anyone I had met in the business. That's where I learned to cheat at gin."

Shirley recalled that director Vincente Minnelli was so meticulous about dressing the sets and scenery that he never used the actors until the last minute.

Of her performance Sinatra said, "She has so much pathos, she can take a piece of comedy and turn it around and make you bust out crying."

Said director Vicente Minnelli: "She can do anything."

Although *Some Came Running* was officially released in 1959 (it premiered January 22, 1959, at Radio City Music Hall in New York City), it had its first review printed in 1958. *Film Daily* had previewed the film on December 17, 1958, and run its review the following day, thus qualifying *Some Came Running* as a 1958 film eligible for Academy Awards at the ceremony in the spring of 1959.

Neither an unhappy Rod Taylor nor a soon-to-be-unhappy Jim Backus makes any headway seducing the virtuous Shirley MacLaine.

Ask Any Girl

Metro-Goldwyn-Mayer / 1959

CREDITS:

Producer, Joe Pasternak; director, Charles Walters; screenplay, George Wells; based on a novel by Winifred Wolfe; music, Jeff Alexander; song, Jimmy McHugh, Dorothy Fields; cinematographer, Robert Bronner; art direction, William A. Horning, Henry Grace; special effects, Robert B. Hoag; editor, John McSweeney, Jr.; recording, Franklin Milton; costumes, Helen Rose; hair styles, Sydney Guilaroff; makeup, William Tuttle. Running time: 98 minutes. MetroColor. CinemaScope.

CAST:

David Niven (*Miles Doughton*); Shirley MacLaine (*Meg Wheeler*); Gig Young (*Evan Doughton*); Rod Taylor (*Ross Taford*); Jim Backus (*Mr. Maxwell*); Claire Kelly (*Lisa*); Elisabeth Fraser (*Jeannie Boyden*); Dody Heath (*Terri Richards*); Read Morgan (*Bert*); Mickey Shaughnessy (*cigarette sampler*); Carmen Phillips (*refined young lady*); Helen Wallace (*hotel manager*); Myrna Hansen, Kasey Rogers, Carrol Byron, Norma French, and Kathy Reed (*girls*).

SYNOPSIS:

Meg Wheeler arrives in Manhattan from a small town. She is in search of a career and a husband. After checking into a hotel for women, she finds a job with a sweater company and quickly falls in love with handsome young executive Ross

Taford. She quickly finds that both her boss and her boyfriend are wolves, and she leaves her job for one in motivational research.

Immediately, she falls in love with her new boss, a super-handsome chap named Evan Doughton. Unfortunately, the feeling is not reciprocal. Evan, ever a bachelor and playboy, prefers many women for many different reasons. Determined to capture her man, Meg decides to use motivational research, and she enlists the aid of Evan's older, more conservative brother, Miles.

Miles borrows his brother's little black address book and personally researches the charms of Evan's girlfriends and relays his findings to Meg, who transforms herself into a composite of all that Evan most desires in women. Armed with this vital information, Meg makes Evan an easy mark, and he quickly proposes.

Meg then discovers that after all, she really desires Miles. Miles lets her know the feeling is mutual.

In love with her playboy boss, Gig Young, Shirley soon discovers the feeling is not mutual.

Shirley, a smalltown girl, plays with a lamb shortly before departing for New York City in search of a husband.

Shirley models a sleeveless evening gown designed for the movie by Academy Award winner Helen Rose.

REVIEWS:

Worth seeing just to watch Miss MacLaine in action. . . . The pert and effervescent actress, who gains increased stature as a performer and a personality with each new outing, again comes through with a performance that is a sheer delight, even topping her Academy Award nomination stint in *Some Came Running*. Her brand of whackiness is contagious and her appeal is unique in that it commands attention among both sexes and all age groups.

Variety

You'll enjoy it while it's going on and after it's over the only thing you'll remember is how talented Miss MacLaine is. She has good looks, good nature, and an elan vital superior to anything poor Bergson ever imagined. I anticipate many happy hours from the comedies I hope she makes in the days of her youth, and from the dramas I'm sure she'll be effective in later on."

Films in Review

With all due regard to the talents and, no doubt, the sterling character of Miss MacLaine, we must say the other young ladies appear more worthy of landing guys than she does. Her vague nonchalance is amusing, but her general defeatist air and her plain lack of chic would seem to place her as that grotesque statistic, one-half a dame.

New York Times

Shirley MacLaine is an extraordinary funny girl. She has the face of an idealized Raggedy Ann, the body of a chorus girl, the dead-eyed, wag-jawed delivery of a ventriloquist's dummy, and she probably possesses beauty, talent and mass appeal in greater degree than any cinema comedienne since Carole Lombard. In recent films *(Hot Spell, Some Came Running)* her somewhat monotonous manner has developed into a supple and imaginative comic style. In *Ask Any Girl* she practices for the first time a sort of I'm-a-grown-up-girl-now decorum and restraint, so that

Shirley models another Helen Rose design—a red-and-black sleeveless coat with patent accents and matching skirt, worn with a jet cashmere sweater.

Shirley and David Niven eventually fall in love and live happily ever after, but first her pencil breaks while she's taking a letter.

when at last she does bust loose, the lulled spectator jumps as if a sleeping hose had suddenly come alive and sputtering.

Time

Since the whole picture is dependent on Miss MacLaine, the principal question must be her personal effectiveness in the role. . . . There are spots where her personality seems dulled by the overly commonplace characterization (that is, by the screenplay) but she manages to keep up to a surprising level of vigor, just the same. . . . The stress is on verve, and verve it generally has, largely owing to Miss MacLaine's enthusiastic hoydenism.

New York Herald Tribune

The poker-faced playing of Mr. Niven set in deliberate contrast to the natural exuberance of Miss MacLaine.

London Times

The combined talents of David Niven and Shirley MacLaine make it a friendly, easy show.

London Observer

Acted with gusto by Niven and Young and happily full of Shirley MacLaine.

London Daily Express

The quiet skill of David Niven and Shirley MacLaine.

Time and Tide

NOTES:

Shirley received the British Film Academy award for Best Actress of 1959 for her role in *Ask Any Girl.* She also received the Silver Bear Award for Best Foreign Actress at the Berlin Film Festival.

This was Shirley's second appearance as costarring love interest to David Niven, and their chemistry here worked as smoothly as it had in *Around the World in 80 Days.*

Mack Sennett called Shirley "the greatest comedienne since Mabel Normand."

Anthony Franciosa and Shirley MacLaine embrace for this studio publicity shot for *Career*.

Career

Paramount / 1959

Producer, Hal Wallis; director, Joseph Anthony; screenplay, James Lee; cinematographer, Joseph La Shelle; associate producer, Paul Nathan; music, Franz Waxman; art direction, Hal Pereira, Walter Tyler; special effects, John P. Fulton; process photography, Farciot Edouart; editor, Warren Low; song, Sammy Cahn, James Van Heusen; costumes, Edith Head; set decoration, Sam Comer, Arthur Krams; makeup, Wally Westmore; hair styles, Nellie Manley. Sound, Gene Merritt, Winston Leverett. Running time: 105 minutes. RegalScope. Black and white.

CAST:

Anthony Franciosa (*Sam Lawson*); Dean Martin (*Maury Novak*); Shirley MacLaine (*Sharon Kensington*); Carolyn Jones (*Shirley Drake*); Joan Blackman (*Barbara*); Robert Middleton (*Robert Kensington*); Donna Douglas (*Marjorie Burke*); Jerry Paris (*Allan Burke*); Frank McHugh (*Charlie*); Chuck Wassil (*Eric Peters*); Mary Treen (*Shirley's secretary*); Allan Hewitt (*Matt Helmsley*); Marjorie Bennett (*columnist*).

SYNOPSIS:

Determined to become a successful actor, Sam Lawson leaves his hometown, moves to a cold-water flat in New York City, and joins a nonpaying off-Broadway drama group formed by Maury Novak, a struggling young director.

A year passes. Sam has married his hometown sweetheart, but his poverty proves too much for her, and after suffering a miscarriage, she returns to their hometown and files for divorce.

Maury in the meantime has found great success as a director. He has become so important that he is unwilling to risk his reputation by hiring an unknown like Sam for a leading role. Taking Maury's advice that only an opportunist can succeed in show business, Sam makes love to, then marries, Maury's alcoholic girlfriend, Sharon Kensington, whose father is a big Broadway producer. When she asks for a divorce in order to marry Maury and have his baby, Sam agrees with the stipulation that he must get the lead in Maury's new play. Maury gives his word but double-crosses Sam by replacing him with a famous Hollywood star.

Sam is drafted, and when he returns from duty in the Korean war, he learns that both he and Maury have been blacklisted because of their earlier association with the off-Broadway theater group.

Though estranged, the two men combine their talents for a new off-Broadway play. The show is a smash hit and quickly moves to Broadway. After fourteen years of lonely struggling, humiliation, and ruthlessness, Sam becomes a star. Shirley Drake, his faithful agent and only true friend, asks him if after all the suffering it was truly worth it. Sam hesitates, but then answers in a firm voice, "Yes, yes, it was worth it."

Shirley, Franciosa, and Joan Blackman share the screen during this party scene.

REVIEWS:

The characters so earnestly portrayed by Anthony Franciosa, Dean Martin, Carolyn Jones and Shirley MacLaine do not grow during the fourteen-year time period of *Career;* they merely gray.

Saturday Review

Miss MacLaine has some misfitting dialogue and story situations to cope with but gets across all right.

Variety

Actor Franciosa gives much the most coherent performance of his career, and he is fairly well supported by Dean Martin and Shirley MacLaine.

Time

Franciosa makes the acquaintance of dipsomaniac Shirley, the thrice-divorced spoiled daughter of a wealthy Broadway producer.

. . . And Shirley MacLaine is as soggy as a dish-rag as a semiprofessional dipsomaniac.

New York Times

NOTES:

Career opened off-Broadway at the Actors Playhouse on April 30, 1957. It was produced by James Preston and Charles Olsen and directed by Olsen. Charles Aidman, Norman Rose, Norma Crane, and Mary James originated the roles played by Franciosa, Martin, MacLaine, and Jones in the film version.

Co-star Carolyn Jones fared better in her role than did Shirley. Jones told *Newsweek* in 1959: "I switched roles with Shirley MacLaine. Shirley wanted to play the drunk kook and I wanted for once to play the straight role. People around here said it was pretty unusual, that they would give their eyeteeth to play the kook. But I figure these roles don't go any place. They're great for comedy or for sex, but if you get stuck with them you're dead. The minute you walk on, the audience labels you a kook and the story has no surprise. I feel that so long as I have to work with corn, fresh corn is better than stale corn."

Jones definitely got the better role in *Career*, proving her insight to be very accurate. For Shirley, it would be years yet before she could live down the kook label completely.

Dean Martin and Shirley, now long married, meet Franciosa outside the theater where the play he's starring in has finally brought him the success for which he's struggled for so long.

Shirley begs husband Franciosa for a divorce, now that she is pregnant from her affair with Dean Martin and wishes to marry him.

Ringleader Frank Sinatra maps out the plan for a big heist. His gang consists of Joey Bishop, Sammy Davis, Jr., Richard Conte, Peter Lawford, and Henry Silva.

Ocean's Eleven

CREDITS:

Producer-director, Lewis Milestone; associate producers, Henry W. Sanicola, Milton Ebbins; story, George Clayton Johnson, Jack Golden Russell; screenplay, Harry Brown, Charles Lederer; assistant director, Ray Gosnell, Jr.; music, Nelson Riddle; art director, Nicolai Remisoff; songs, Sammy Cahn and James Van Heusen; cinematography, William H. Daniels; editor, Philip W. Anderson. Panavision. Technicolor. Running time: 127 minutes.

CAST:

Frank Sinatra (*Danny Ocean*); Dean Martin (*Sam Harmon*); Sammy Davis, Jr. (*Josh Howard*); Peter Lawford (*Jimmy Foster*); Angie Dickinson (*Beatrice Ocean*); Richard Conte (*Anthony Bergdorf*); Cesar Romero (*Duke Santos*); Patrice Wymore (*Adele Ekstrom*); Joey Bishop (*Mush O'Conners*); Akim Tamiroff (*Spyros Acebos*); Henry Silva (*Roger Corneal*); Ilka Chase (*Mrs. Restes*); Buddy Lester (*Vincent Massler*); Richard Benedict (*Curly Steffens*); Jean Willes (*Mrs. Bergdorf*); Norman Fell (*Peter Rheimer*); Clem Harvey (*Louis Jackson*); Hank Henry (*Mr. Kelly*); Charles Meredith (*Mr. Cohen*); Anne Neyland (*Delores*); Joan Staley (*Helen*); George E. Stone (*proprietor*); Marjorie Bennett (*customer*); Louis Quinn (*De Wolfe*); Laura Cornell (*Sugarface*); John Indrisano (*Texan*); Shiva (*snake dancer*); Steve Pendleton (*Major Taylor*); Ronnie Dapo (*Timmy*); Carmen Phillips (*hungry girl*); Paul Bryar (*police officer*); Red Skelton (*client*); John Craven (*cashier*); Lew Gallo (*jealous young man*); John Holland (*man*); Shirley MacLaine (*drunk girl*); Barbara Sterling (*girl*); Murray Alper (*deputy*); Tom

Shirley MacLaine laughs it up with Sammy Davis, Jr., during a break in filming.

Middleton (*TV newsman*); Hoot Gibson (*roadblock deputy*); Sparky Kaye (*Riviera manager*); Forrest Lederer (*Sands manager*); George Raft (*Jack Strager*); Rummy Bishop (*Castleman*); Gregory Gay (*Freeman*); Don "Red" Barry (*McCoy*); William Justine (*Parelli*).

SYNOPSIS:

Ten former U.S. 82nd Airborne Commandos, headed by Danny Ocean (Sinatra), plot an ingenious robbery of five Las Vegas gambling casinos simultaneously at midnight New Year's Eve. With precision timing they explode an electrical tower, blacking out the whole city and leaving the electronically controlled money vaults vulnerable.

The holdup goes off exactly as planned. The money, deposited in garbage cans outside the robbed casinos, is picked up by Josh Howard (Sammy Davis, Jr.) in his garbage truck.

One of the men, Anthony Bergdorf (Richard Conte), dies in the street of a heart attack, thus complicating the gang's mission to get the loot out of Las Vegas. The gang then manages

Shirley plays a decidedly tipsy lady in her now-famous cameo with Dean Martin in *Ocean's 11*.

to hide the loot in Bergdorf's coffin, little realizing that Bergdorf's widow has arranged for her husband's cremation.

During the ceremony Ocean and his gang watch mournfully as their friend and their loot go up in flames.

REVIEWS:

Frank Sinatra heads the list of big names in the line-up, followed by clan regulars Dean Martin, Peter Lawford and Sammy Davis Jr., not to mention Shirley MacLaine who does an unbilled bit as an inebriated New Year's Eve celebrant.

Los Angeles Mirror

NOTES:

While making *The Apartment* for Billy Wilder, Shirley took a brief break—long enough to fly up to Las Vegas to do a cameo in *Ocean's 11*. In her bit, Shirley plays a drunken floozie who, after emerging from her car and losing her key, bends over to search for it and then can't straighten up.

When Dean Martin comes to her rescue, Shirley grabs him and plants a sloppy kiss on him. When they both straighten up, Shirley's giggle turns to a disappointed frown as she realizes that Martin wants nothing to with her.

"It's a dirty deal," she slobbers. "I don't fit into your picture, huh?"

Preoccupied with the heist he's trying to pull, Martin retorts, "From here on in you don't, sweetheart."

To which Shirley quickly replies, "It so happens, I'm very much in demand."

The take took less than five minutes for a satisfactory print.

Youthful crusading magistrate Louis Jourdan comes to Montmarte to investigate the scandalous can-can, finds nightclub owner Shirley MacLaine, and instantly falls in love with her.

Can-Can

20th Century-Fox / 1960

CREDITS:

Producer, Jack Cummings; associate producer, Saul Chapin; director, Walter Lang; based on the play by Abe Burrows and Cole Porter; screenplay, Dorothy Kingsley, Charles Lederer; music, Nelson Riddle; songs, Cole Porter; art direction, Lyle Wheeler, Jack Martin Smith; choreography, Hermes Pan; cinematographer, William H. Daniels; editor, Robert Simpson. Running time: 131 minutes. Todd-AO. Technicolor.

CAST:

Frank Sinatra *(François Durnais)*; Shirley MacLaine *(Simone Pistache)*; Maurice Chevalier *(Paul Barriere)*; Louis Jourdan *(Philippe Forrestier)*; Juliet Prowse *(Claudine)*; Marcel Dalio *(André—headwaiter)*; Leon Belasco *(Arturo—orchestra leader)*; Jean Del Val *(Judge Merceaux)*; John A. Neris *(photographer)*; Eugene Borden *(Chevrolet)*; Jonathan Kidd *(recorder)*; Marc Wilder *(Adam)*; Peter Coe *(policeman Dupont)*; Marcel de la Proesse *(plainclothesman)*; Renee Godfrey, Lili Valenty *(dowagers)*; Charles Carmen *(knife thrower)*; Carole Bryan *(Gigi)*; Barbara Carter *(Camille)*; Jane Earl *(Renée)*; Ruth Earl *(Julie)*; Laura Fraser *(Germaine)*; Vera Lee *(Gabrielle)*; Lisa Mitchell *(Fifi)*; Wanda Shannon *(Maxine)*; Wilda Taylor *(Lili)*; Darlene Tittle *(Gisele)*; Ambrogio Malerba *(apache dancer)*; Alphonse Martell *(butler)*; Genevieve Aumont *(secretary)*; Edward Le Veque *(judge)*; Maurice Marsac, Nestor Paiva *(bailiffs)*.

SYNOPSIS:

Ancient French statute has forbidden the dancing of the can-can. Lawyer François Durnais (Frank

Lawyer Frank Sinatra and judge Maurice Chevalier hide behind waiters' aprons to avoid arrest when the cabaret owned by Shirley MacLaine is raided by police.

Sinatra) uses his influence with his friend Judge Paul Barriere (Maurice Chevalier) to keep police from closing down the café of his girlfriend, Simone Pistache (Shirley MacLaine).

New barrister Philippe Forrestier (Louis Jourdan) tries to get Simone's café raided and her dancers arrested, but while visiting the café to plan his raid, he falls in love with Simone and proposes marriage. Simone does not reciprocate, because she loves François, from whom she tries to wangle a proposal.

François believes that love and marriage cannot be mixed and will not say the proper words to Simone. Simone then plans to use Philippe's proposal as a threat to François.

Meanwhile, Barriere and François scheme to have Simone embarrass Philippe in front of his socialite friends. The scheme works, but Philippe, still undaunted, proposes marriage to Simone once more. François is now forced into a counter-

In "The Garden of Eden" ballet sequence, Shirley portrays Eve to Marc Wilder's Adam.

Shirley MacLaine (right) and Juliet Prowse (left forground) go through the strenuous paces of the can-can dance sequence

In a Parisian courtroom where Frank Sinatra is being tried, Shirley will not, when asked, produce evidence that will help convict him

proposal, which is accepted by Simone. The can-can is legalized shortly after a special performance before the court.

REVIEWS:

Miss MacLaine—grisette, gamine and cocotte rolled into one continuous explosion—comes off more spectacularly than Sinatra.

Los Angeles Times

The erratic Miss MacLaine acts as though she had a patent on personality, and clearly needs a hard-hearted director who would dare to disillusion her now and then.

Newsweek

Shirley MacLaine is such a natural clown, and seems to be so benignly an extroverted gal, you don't really care she is totally un-French.

Films in Review

The mingling of Miss MacLaine and Frank Sinatra's very American American accents with the French of Chevalier and Jourdan is surprisingly not as incongruous as one might expect. Miss MacLaine can whang out a line like "I'm

Shirley high-kicking the can-can. Though more athletic than provocative, the can-can was considered shocking in the 1890s.

A publicity shot of a happy trio, Frank Sinatra, Shirley MacLaine, and Maurice Chevalier.

surprised the word doesn't turn to stone in your mouth" with the clang of a tin cup on an anvil.

New York Herald Tribune

Star MacLaine, who with better direction has handled herself like an American Kay Kendall, seems little better in this picture than a female Jerry Lewis.

Time

Miss MacLaine is bouncy, outgoing, scintillating, vivacious, and appealing . . . but French she ain't. . . . The dance numbers for the most part are the highlights of the film, most particularly Miss MacLaine's apache dance.

Variety

The best—or let's say, the least ennuying—of these is a fast apache thing in which four rather violent young fellows play beanbag with Shirley MacLaine. She being suited to that purpose and not very nimble on her feet. . . . Chevalier totters meekly on the fringes as an elderly judge who in this picture is not so sure that God should be thanked for little girls particularly when the creatures are as frightening as Miss MacLaine.

New York Times

NOTES:

The Songs: "Montmarte" (Sinatra and Chevalier); "Maidens Typical of France" (chorus); "C'est magnifique" (Sinatra and MacLaine); "Live and Let Live" (Chevalier and Jourdan); "It's All Right with Me" (Sinatra); "Let's Do It" (Sinatra and MacLaine); "Just One of Those

Shirley MacLaine with director Walter Lang, on the set of *Can-Can,* during a break from the "Garden of Eden" ballet sequence.

Things" (Chevalier); "You Do Something to Me" (Jourdan); "I Love Paris" (Chorus).

The Dances: "Maidens Typical of France," "Apache," "The Garden of Eden Ballet," and "Can-can."

Can-Can opened on Broadway at the Schubert Theatre on May 7, 1953. Feuer and Martin produced, the book and direction were by Abe Burrows, and Michael Kidd was the choreographer. Lilo, Gwen Verdon, Peter Cookson, and C. K. Alexander originated the roles played by MacLaine, Prowse, Jourdan, and Chevalier in the film.

The screenplay departs radically from the original book; in fact, the character played by Sinatra was not in the Broadway show. Many of the original songs: "Never Give Anything Away," "I Am in Love," "If You Loved Me Truly," "Allez-Vous En," "Never, Never Be an Artist," "Every Man Is a Stupid Man" have been dropped from the film, and "I Love Paris" is merely used as background music.

On the other hand, three old Cole Porter songs have been added: "Let's Do It," "Just One of Those Things," and "You Do Something to Me."

The film received worldwide publicity when Russian Premier Nikita Khrushchev visited the 20th Century-Fox lot during a visit to the United States. After watching a performance of the can-can he remarked: "Immoral. . . . The face of humanity is more beautiful than its backside."

Shirley, as elevator operator Fran Kubelik, is convulsed during an office party as Ray Walston, with garters, dances on a table.

The Apartment

United Artists / 1960

CREDITS:

Producer-director, Billy Wilder; associate producers, Doane Harrison, I. A. L. Diamond; screenplay, Billy Wilder, I. A. L. Diamond; assistant director, Hal Polaire; art director, Alexander Trauner; music, Adolph Deutsch; songs, Adolph Deutsch, Charles Williams; cinematographer, Joseph LaShelle; editor, Daniel Mandell. Running time: 125 minutes. Panavision. Black and white.

CAST:

Jack Lemmon *(C. C. "Bud" Baxter)*; Shirley MacLaine *(Fran Kubelik)*; Fred MacMurray *(Jeff D. Scheldrake)*; Ray Walston *(Joe Dobisch)*; David Lewis *(Al Kirkeby)*; Jack Kruschen *(Dr. Dreyfuss)*; Joan Shawlee *(Sylvia)*; Edie Adams *(Miss Olsen)*; Hope Holiday *(Margie MacDougall)*; Johnny Seven *(Karl Matuschka)*; Naomi Stevens *(Mrs. Dreyfuss)*; Frances Weintraub Lax *(Mrs. Lieberman)*; Joyce Jameson *(the blonde)*; Willard Waterman *(Mr. Vanderhof)*; David White *(Mr. Eichelberger)*; Benny Burt *(bartender)*; Hal Smith *(Santa Claus)*; Dorothy Abbott *(office worker)*.

SYNOPSIS:

C. C. Baxter is a mild-mannered but ambitious computer operator in a giant Manhattan insurance company. To ingratiate himself with his four philandering department heads, he allows

Fred MacMurray is excellent as J. D. Sheldrake, a heel of an executive who promises Shirley that eventually he'll leave his wife for her, but he never does.

them the use of his bachelor apartment for their extramarital affairs. His payoff comes quickly when he is promoted to assistant to the company's top man, J. D. Sheldrake, who also desires use of C. C.'s apartment. Baxter is quickly disillusioned when he discovers that Sheldrake is entertaining lovely elevator operator Fran Kubelik, whom Baxter had hoped to win for himself.

After the Christmas Eve office party Baxter returns home, to find Fran overdosed on sleeping pills, which the unhappy woman took when she realized Sheldrake never had any intention of divorcing his wife to marry her. With help from his kindly doctor neighbor, Baxter revives the distraught Fran and allows her to stay in his apartment until she is recovered.

A few days later, Sheldrake demands use of the apartment for a New Year's Eve party with Fran. Emphatically refusing to allow this in his pad, Baxter quits his job. When Fran learns of the incident, she realizes how Baxter must love her, and she races to his apartment to comfort him and remain with him for good.

REVIEWS:

Shirley MacLaine makes the elevator girl, who fornicates with MacMurray in Lemmon's bed, more attractive than such a girl would be in real life.

Films in Review

A splendid performance by Shirley MacLaine.

New York Times

Director Wilder handles his players superbly. He holds an amazingly tight rein on actress MacLaine, which gives her performance a solidity she seldom achieves.

Time

Miss MacLaine has never been more enticing, more forlorn, more a girl you would like to help no matter what the hazards, a girl for whom you would risk job, future, past, happy home, what-have-you.

New York Post

[Her] neurotically debonair elevator girl is as subtle a piece of work as she has turned in so far.

New York Herald Tribune

Again in pixie hairdo, [she] is a prize that's consistent with the fight being waged for her affection. Her ability to play it broad where it should be broad, subtle where it must be subtle, enables the actress to effect reality and yet do much more. Rather than a single human being, Miss MacLaine symbolizes the universal prey, of convincing conniving men within the glass walls of commerce.

Variety

Miss MacLaine and Mr. Lemmon work their heads off to achieve "sincere" portrayals, and Edie Adams and Fred MacMurray give accomplished performances in subordinate roles.

Saturday Review

NOTES:

Shirley received her second Academy Award nomination, for Best Actress of 1960, losing to Elizabeth Taylor for *Butterfield 8*. Shirley was named Best Actress at the 1960 Venice Film Festival for her portrayal of Fran Kubelik.

Shirley recalls in *Don't Fall off the Mountain*, "*The Apartment* had just been released and was well received. A man walked over to me and introduced himself as an interpreter for Mr. Khrushchev while he was at the United Nations and said he had a message from the

After Shirley's suicide attempt, Jack Kruschen and Jack Lemmon try to keep her awake, to counter the effect of the sleeping pills she has taken.

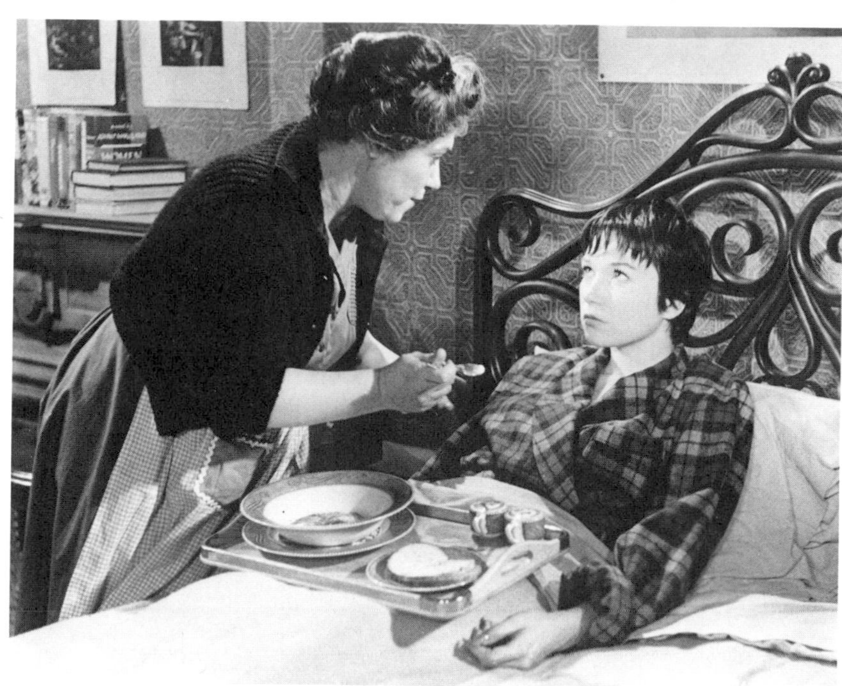

Naomi Stevens, Lemmon's next-door neighbor, feeds hot chicken soup to Shirley, who has begun to recover.

Premier. . . . 'The Premier sends his regards, wishes to be remembered to you, and says he's just seen your new picture, *The Apartment,* and you've improved.' "

One of director Billy Wilder's idiosyncrasies is to start without finishing the script. The final scene of *The Apartment* was filmed within fifteen minutes after the arrival of mimeographed pages on the set, with Jack Lemmon and Shirley MacLaine having to learn their lines from warm, wet copies.

The office Christmas-party sequence was actually shot on December 23, 1959. Wilder's stars and more than 250 extras got the shot printed on the first take. Wilder later remarked: "Who needs a director? I just say, 'Action!' and stand back."

Shirley later told *Time* magazine: "Working

Jack Lemmon, secretly in love with Shirley tries to cheer her out of her depression.

Shirley mugs for the camera as Jack Lemmon has a makeup adjustment in the background.

with Billy was like one long ten-week acting lesson. He can be as disciplined as a soldier and as soft as velvet."

Reflecting on working with Wilder on *The Apartment* Shirley told Britain's *Films and Filming* magazine: "Billy Wilder has a complete blueprint for a film before he starts shooting. He's very dominating. He knows what he wants and he's absolutely certain. It's not that he leaves the actor out of it. We can discuss things with Wilder and come to some kind of agreement. Once you get on the set the important things for Billy are the script and the first preview. What happens on the set is unimportant compared to the other two, because the script is such a polished product that he knows exactly how it will work."

Shirley, as the elevator girl, clowns with director Billy Wilder as Jack Lemmon looks on.

A shocked Shirley reacts to Dean Martin's hidden tape recorder as a puzzled Cliff Robertson watches.

All in a Night's Work

Paramount / 1961

CREDITS:

Producer, Hal Wallis; director, Joseph Anthony; based on a story by Margit Veszi and a play by Owen Elford; screenplay, Edmund Beloin, Maurice Richlin, Sidney Shelton; cinematographer, Joseph La Shelle; art direction, Hal Pereira, Walter Tyler; set decoration, Sam Comer, Arthur Krams; editor, Howard Smith; music, Andre Previn; sound, Gene Merritt; costumes, Edith Head; makeup, Wally Westmore; hair styles, Nellie Manley; process photography, Farciot Edouart; special effects, John P. Fulton. Running time: 94 minutes. Technicolor.

CAST:

Dean Martin *(Tony Ryder)*; Shirley MacLaine *(Katie Robbins)*; Cliff Robertson *(Warren Kingsley, Jr.)*; Charles Ruggles *(Warren Kingsley, Sr.)*; Norma Crane *(Marge Coombs)*; Jack Weston

Shirley, naked beneath her towel, flees down a corridor, with hotel detective Jack Weston in hot pursuit.

After filling Shirley with champagne, Dean tries to seduce her, but somehow she ends up on top of him.

(Lasker); Gale Gordon *(Oliver Dunning)*; Jerome Cowan *(Sam Weaver)*; Mabel Albertson *(Mrs. Kingsley, Sr.)*; Mary Treen *(Miss Schuster)*; Charles Evans *(Colonel Ryder)*; Gertrude Astor *(customer)*; John Hudson *(Harry Lane)*; Ralph Dumke *(Baker)*; Roy Gordon *(Albright)*; Ian Wolfe *(O'Hara)*; Rex Evans *(Carter)*.

SYNOPSIS:

While on vacation in Palm Beach, Katie Robbins, a researcher for a New York publishing firm, saves a drunken millionaire from drowning. When she removes her soaked clothing, however, the grateful millionaire becomes amorously revived so that Katie must flee from his advances. Dressed only in a towel and a pair of earrings, she darts into a nearby room and finds a man lying on a bed with a blissful smile on his face. As she races back down the corridor she is spied by the house detective, who gives chase. Though he loses track of Katie, he does find one of her earrings.

Unknown to Katie, the man in the bed was the head of her publishing company, and he was dead. Playboy Tony Ryder inherits the company and is promptly warned that the firm will probably be blackmailed by the mystery woman seen fleeing the old boss's hotel room. Once Tony spots Katie with the missing earring he jumps to the wrong conclusion and attempts to thwart any blackmail attempts by awarding Katie a two-hundred-dollar-a-week raise. Furthermore, he tries to speed up her marriage to an antiseptic veterinarian, Dr. Warren Kingsley, Jr., hoping that once Katie's settled down she will ease up on the blackmail demands. When his scheme backfires, Tony invites Katie to his apartment for dinner. After filling her with champagne and romantic innuendo, he announces he is willing to forgive her for trying to blackmail the firm. Furious, Katie stamps out. Tony then realizes her innocence and his love for her and goes after her.

REVIEWS:

Miss MacLaine is still playing the sweet, naïve, tanglefooted kook she began a few years back in *Some Came Running,* but she plays it with such innocent sincerity and comic gusto that she thoroughly succeeds in winning over the audience and gives the film a much needed shot in the funny-bone.

Variety

Miss MacLaine and Mr. Martin spar and weave with a great deal more determination than the plot seems to justify.

New York Times

In *All in a Night's Work* Shirley MacLaine is in her comedic guise, and her flair for racy innocence has much to do with making a relatively standardized story come off with reasonably comic grace. . . . She can fling herself into slapstick without losing one whit of her characterization, can live in perpetual draft of confusion without losing her balance. . . . She has a mastery of the sort of optimistic daze that has more than a blood relationship with the classic screen comedians of yesterday. . . . It is farce, but good farce, and Miss MacLaine adds a freshness of performance that gives it the illusion if not the substance of originality.

Films in Review

NOTES:

The source for this farce of double entendres is an unidentified play by Owen Elford and an unidentified story by Margit Veszi.

Secretary Shirley's favorite position for taking steno from handsome playboy boss Dean Martin.

Though playing a frigid spinster schoolmarm, lovely Shirley still manages to look quite sexy and certainly miscast.

Two Loves

Metro-Goldwyn-Mayer / 1961

CREDITS:

Producer, Julian Blaustein; director, Charles Walters; based on the novel *Spinster,* by Sylvia Ashton-Warner; screenplay, Ben Maddow; art direction, George W. Favis, Urie McCleary; music, Bronislau Kaper; assistant director, William Shanks; special effects, Robert R. Hoag, Lee LeBlanc; cinematographer, Joseph Ruttenberg; editor, Frederic Stunkamp. Running time: 100 minutes. Metrocolor. CinemaScope.

CAST:

Shirley MacLaine *(Anna)*; Laurence Harvey *(Paul)*; Jack Hawkins *(Abercrombie)*; Nobu McCarthy *(Whareparita)*; Ronald Long *(Headmaster Reardon)*; Norah Howard *(Mrs. Cutter)*; Juano Hernandez *(Rauhuia)*; Edmund Vargas *(Matawhero)*; Neil Woodward *(Mark Cutter)*; Lisa Sitjar *(Hinewaka)*; Alan Roberts *(Seven)*.

SYNOPSIS:

American-born Anna Vorontosov is a schoolteacher in a remote, primitive section of New Zealand. Her unorthodox teaching methods (she casts aside prescribed textbooks) have won her

Shirley finds her fellow teacher Laurence Harvey neurotic yet attractive.

the admiration and affection of her young students and their parents as well as the admiration of the school inspector, Abercrombie. Her personal life, however, is fraught with turmoil. Frightened of love and sexually inhibited, she has always remained aloof and frigid in her relations with men. Eager to break down this barrier is fellow teacher Paul Lathrope, a somewhat irrational and immature man. Though Anna finds herself attracted to him, she is unable to submit to his advances.

One day, she is shocked to learn that one of her native helpers, a fifteen-year-old Maori girl called Whareparita, is expecting a child. Equally devastating to Anna is the realization that both the young woman and her parents are eagerly awaiting the new arrival. This simple acceptance of nature, coupled with Paul's con-

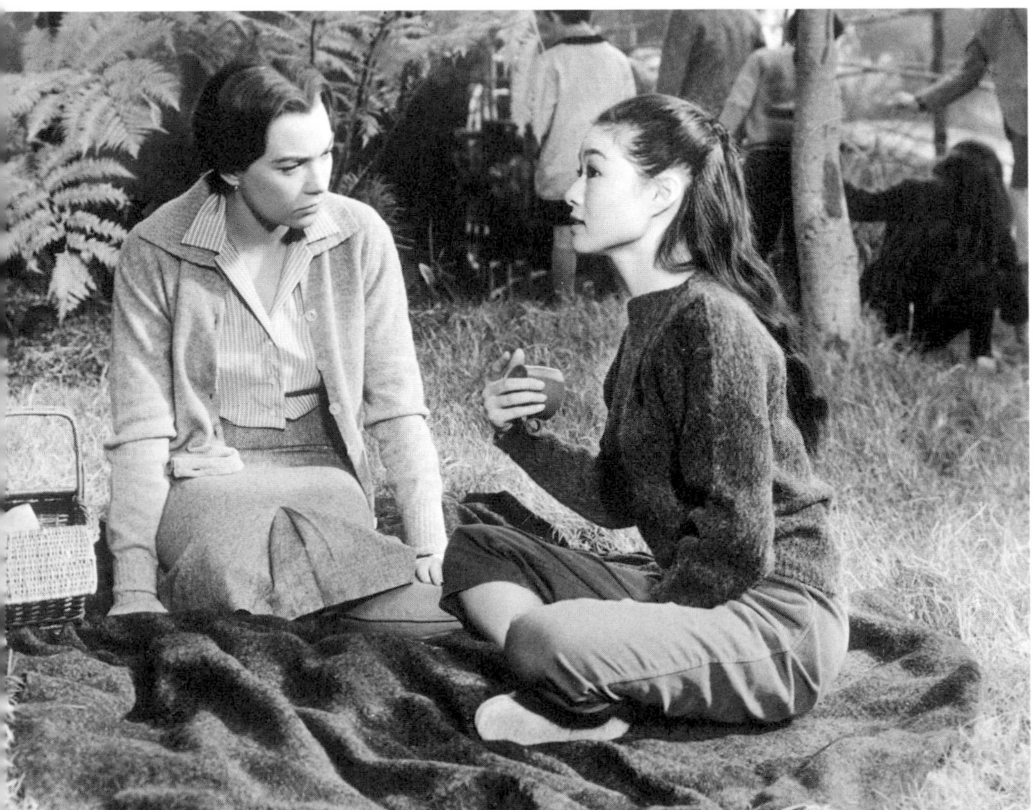

As the sexually repressed schoolteacher, Shirley is shocked to learn that her fifteen-year-old assistant, played by Nobu McCarthy, is pregnant.

Shirley freezes as Laurence Harvey attempts to seduce her.

stant advances, so disturbs Anna that she begins to question her own way of life.

Suddenly, tragically, Whareparita's child dies at birth, and Paul is killed in a motorcycle accident—possibly suicide. Shortly before Paul's funeral Anna learns it was Paul who fathered Whareparita's dead child. Overcome by guilt, Anna blames her frigidity for the tragic turn of events. Only when Abercrombie convinces her that no person is directly responsible for the actions of someone else, is Anna able to absolve herself of the terrible guilt she has carried. And now, encouraged by the gentle and understanding love offered by Abercrombie, Anna finally realizes she has nothing to fear from life.

REVIEWS:

Miss MacLaine, although not ideally suited to the role, manages for the most part to rise above the miscasting and deliver an interesting performance.

Variety

Miss MacLaine's underlying good-natured charm go away long enough to make her occasional spasms of anguish seem credible.

New York Herald Tribune

Shirley MacLaine's performance is matter-of-fact, energetic and competent but not over-burdened with nuances.

New York Times

Director Charles Walters should have declined the assignment. So should Miss MacLaine.

Films in Review

Shirley finally accepts the understanding love of the older, more mature Jack Hawkins at the film's end.

NOTES:

Based on the novel *Spinster,* by New Zealand author Sylvia Ashton-Warner, the film was released in Britain under that title. The action takes place in New Zealand, but the entire film was shot in and around Southern California.

Shirley MacLaine has referred to *Two Loves* as "an unfortunate film." Having chosen the script herself to fulfill a contractual commitment to MGM, Shirley must not not have paid close attention to the lack of depth and to the character motivations that were so poorly, if at all, realized in the filmed product.

Variety pointed out: "[MacLaine] is presented as a self-sufficient woman seemingly quite content to thrust herself into her work. Yet the story is bent on proving she is an unhappy, incomplete woman."

Shirley and Audrey Hepburn portray headmistresses of a small, exclusive boarding school for wealthy girls.

The Children's Hour

United Artists / 1962

CREDITS:

Producer, William Wyler; associate producer, Robert Wyler; director, William Wyler; screenplay, John Michael Hayes; adaptation, Lillian Hellman, based on her play; music, Alex North; cinematographer, Franz F. Planer; art direction, Fernando Carrere; set decoration, Edward G. Boyle; editor, Robert Swink; sound, Fred Lau, Don Hall, Jr.; costumes, Dorothy Jeakins; make-up, Emile La Vigne, Frank McCoy. Running time: 107 minutes. Black and white.

CAST:

Audrey Hepburn (*Karen Wright*); Shirley MacLaine (*Martha Dobie*); James Garner (*Dr. Joe Cardin*); Miriam Hopkins (*Mrs. Lily Mortar*); Fay Bainter (*Mrs. Amelia Tilford*); Karen Balkin (*Mary Tilford*); Veronica Cartwright (*Rosalie*); Jered Barclay (*grocery boy*).

SYNOPSIS:

Karen Wright and Martha Dobie are the headmistresses for a small private school for girls. Their major problem is ill-disciplined twelve-year-old Mary Tilford, granddaughter of the small town's most influential citizen. One day, when the child is punished for lying, she rushes home to her grandmother and tells another lie, more terrible and damaging than the first. She accuses her two teachers of having an "unnatural" relationship.

Although the child herself only barely perceives what she has stated, the effect on her

Shirley MacLaine in one of her best performances as the guilt-ridden, troubled Martha Dobie in *The Children's Hour*.

Accompanied by James Garner, who plays Hepburn's fiancé, these three visit the grandmother of the child who has accused Audrey and Shirley of having an unnatural relationship.

grandmother is swift and shocking, and the little girl quickly elaborates on her story. Horrified, grandmother Tilford speedily removes her child from the school and urges all other parents and guardians to do the same.

Karen and Martha, scandalized, bring a slander suit against Mrs. Tilford but lose the much-publicized court trial when their chief witness, Martha's irresponsible Aunt Lily, deserts under pressure and refuses to testify on their behalf.

Not only is the school destroyed but Karen realizes that Mary's lie has even succeeded in tainting the love of her fiancé, Dr. Joe Cardin. After sending him away, she suggests to Martha that they go somewhere new and try to rebuild their lives. But the scandal has aroused in Martha the terrible realization that the lie touched upon a hidden truth, and she hysterically confesses her love for Karen. Then, ill with despair, she hangs herself.

The vicious lie is eventually exposed, but

At the house of Fay Bainter (extreme left) Shirley, Garner, and Hepburn await the arrival of the youthful accuser.

Young Karen Balkin stands firm as she repeats her accusation in front of the shocked Hepburn and MacLaine.

for Karen it is too late. Following Martha's funeral, she walks silently past Joe, Mrs. Tilford, and the other repentant townspeople.

REVIEWS:

Shirley MacLaine, all forlorn, gives the best performance of her career as the teacher who is sickened to find that she is partly homosexual. She gives viewers a touching and indelible lesson in what cinema acting is all about.

Time

Shirley MacLaine inclines to be too kittenish in some scenes and do too much vocal handwringing toward the end.

New York Times

The personalities of Audrey Hepburn and Shirley MacLaine beautifully complement each other. Miss Hepburn's soft sensitivity, marvelous projection and emotional understatement result in a memorable portrayal. Miss MacLaine's enact-

Young Karen Balkin is questioned by Garner about her accusation as Bainter, MacLaine, and Hepburn watch and listen.

ment is almost equally rich in depth and substance.

Variety

Always a perfectionist [Wyler] obtains top performances from every one of his principals (although in the interest of verisimilitude, Hepburn and MacLaine might well have switched roles).

Saturday Review

What makes Miss MacLaine's performance so much more trenchant is that while Miss Hepburn is asked to portray little more than disbelief, defiance and the posture of pride, Miss MacLaine is absolutely involved. Her scene of horrible and fatal self-reproach is the most affecting psychological event in the picture and its dramatic high point.

New York Herald Tribune

Shirley confronts the little girl, but malicious Karen Balkin holds fast to her tale.

NOTES:

The play first opened on Broadway at the Maxine Elliott Theatre on November 20, 1934. Herman Shumlin produced and directed, Katherine Emery was Karen, Anne Revere (Academy Award winner) was Martha, Robert Keith was Joe, Katherine Emmet was Mrs. Tilford, and Florence McGee was Mary.

The movie rights were purchased by Samuel Goldwyn but the Hays Office insisted the title be changed and all references to Lesbianism be omitted. Under the title *These Three* (1936), the film version changed the Lesbian theme to adultery and was both a critical and a commercial success. Wyler also directed this version, Miss Hellman did the adaptation, Merle Oberon was Karen, Miriam Hopkins was Martha (she played Aunt Lily in this version), Joel McCrea was Joe, Alma Kruger was Mrs. Tilford, and Bonita Granville was Mary.

As their court trial comes to an end, Shirley and Audrey realize they are going to lose their slander suit. Carl Benton Reid portrays the trial judge.

Troubled and full of self-hate, Shirley admits her confused feelings of love to Audrey Hepburn. Shortly thereafter, Shirley commits suicide.

The play was revived on Broadway at the Coronet Theatre on December 18, 1952. Kermit Bloomgarden produced, Hellman directed, Kim Hunter was Karen, Patricia Neal was Martha, Robert Pastene was Joe, Emmet was again Mrs. Tilford, and Iris Mann was Mary.

The film opened in Los Angeles in December in order to be eligible for 1961 Academy Awards and received five nominations: Supporting Actress (Fay Bainter), Art Direction (black and white film), Photography (black and white film), Costumes (black and white film), and Sound.

Shirley remembers: "I should have fought more with Billy Wyler to investigate the Lesbian relationship. In one scene I baked a cake for [Audrey Hepburn], cut it like a work of art, placed the doilies just so. Every nuance was the act of a lover. There were several scenes like that, but Wyler was afraid, so they were cut from the script the day before we started shooting. And I'd built the concept of my character on precisely those scenes."

Hepburn tells MacLaine that she has just broken her engagement to Garner.

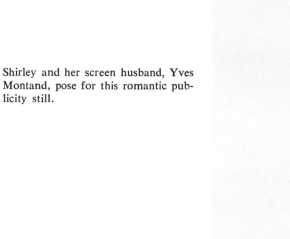

Shirley and her screen husband, Yves Montand, pose for this romantic publicity still.

My Geisha

Paramount / 1962

CREDITS:

Producer, Steve Parker; director, Jack Cardiff; screenplay, Norman Krasna; music, Franz Waxman; song, Franz Waxman, Hal David; assistant director, Harry Kratz; art direction, Hal Pereira, Arthur Lonegan, Makoto Kikuchi; cinematographer, Shunichuo Nakao; editor, Archie Marshek. Running time: 119 minutes. Technirama. Color. Filmed in Japan.

CAST:

Shirley MacLaine *(Lucy Dell/Yoko Mori)*; Yves Montand *(Paul Robaix)*; Bob Cummings *(Bob Moore)*; Edward G. Robinson *(Sam Lewis)*; Yoko Tani *(Kazumi Ito)*; Tatsuo Saito *(Kenichi Takata);* Alex Gerry *(Leonard Lewis)*; Nobuo Chiba *(Shig)*; Ichiro Hayakawa *(Hisako Amatsu)*; George Furness *(George)*.

SYNOPSIS:

Irritated because he is known merely as the director of his wife, Lucy's, films, Paul Robaix decides to go to Japan and make a "new wave" film starring an unknown geisha in Puccini's *Madame Butterfly*. The outraged Lucy, accompanied by producer Sam Lewis, follows Paul to Japan and disguises herself, under black wig, white powder, and kimono, as a geisha.

When Paul fails to recognize her, she as-

Shirley MacLaine as a geisha, Yoko Mori, in full costume and makeup, with brown contact lenses covering her bright blue eyes.

Shirley and Yoko Tani are accompanied to a sumo-wrestling match by Edward G. Robinson, Yves Montand, and Bob Cummings.

sumes the name of Yoko Mori, takes lessons from a true geisha named Kazumi, passes a screen test, and becomes Paul's new discovery.

Complications arise when her wolf of a leading man, Bob Moore, falls in love with her and asks Paul to help him win her hand. Shortly before filming is completed, Paul accidentally discovers the deception. Deeply hurt, he feels Lucy has deprived him of his one chance to win recognition without her support. But when *Madame Butterfly* is premiered in Tokyo, Lucy, now wise in the ways of a geisha, appears as herself and tells the applauding audience that Yoko Mori has entered a convent and retired from the screen. She then proudly introduces her husband and gives him the entire credit for the film.

Shirley is accompanied on her trip to Japan by her producer, Sam Lewis, played by expert scene stealer Edward G. Robinson.

Famous makeup artist Frank Westmore applies the complex and very painful eye tabs that give Shirley her oriental look.

Shirley darkens her eyebrows after applying the geisha-white face powder that completely hid her freckles.

REVIEWS:

Shirley MacLaine is more subdued than normal and contributes a performance in keeping with the stylized, formal nature of the geisha. She appears, above all, at ease in the role.

New York Times

Miss MacLaine gives her customary spirited portrayal, yet skillfully submerges her unpredictably gregarious personality into that of the dainty tranquil geisha for the bulk of the proceedings.

Variety

I am willing enough to be fascinated by Miss MacLaine.

New York Herald Tribune

Some hilarious lowbrow farce sequences help, as do the handsomely photographed Japanese landscapes, and the clowning of Shirley MacLaine as the false geisha, and Bob Cummings as a male Hollywood sex bomb who takes his work seriously.

Show

At the film's end, Shirley is happily united with her husband, Yves Montand, and their project together is a triumph.

Omaha lawyer Robert Mitchum meets Bronx Jewish dancer Shirley MacLaine at a party in Greenwich Village.

Two for the Seesaw

United Artists / 1962

CREDITS:

Producer, Walter Mirisch; director, Robert Wise; based on a play by William Gibson; screenplay, Isobel Lennart; music, Andre Previn; assistant director, Jerome M. Siegel; cinematographer, Ted McCord; editor, Stuart Gilmore. Running time: 119 minutes. Panavision. Black and white.

CAST:

Robert Mitchum *(Jerry Ryan)*; Shirley MacLaine *(Gittel Mosca)*; Edmond Ryan *(Taubman)*; Elisabeth Fraser *(Sophie)*; Eddie Firestone *(Oscar)*; Billy Gray *(Mr. Jacoby)*.

SYNOPSIS:

Following the breakup of his marriage and the subsequent loss of his job, Jerry Ryan, a lawyer from Omaha, arrives in Manhattan. While visiting a friend in Greenwich Village, he meets Gittel Mosca, a Bronx-bred dance enuthusiast. Almost immediately a warm friendship develops between the oddly matched pair, and for Gittel it eventually ripens into love. But Jerry's thoughts are still in Omaha, and he is unable to give completely of himself. He does, however, get a job with a fine law firm and uses some of his money to set Gittel up with a little dance studio in an empty loft. And when she has to be operated upon for a hemorrhaging ucler, Jerry devotedly cares for her.

The time finally arrives when Gittel feels

marriage is the inevitable next step, and she asks Jerry to make her his wife. Gittel quickly realizes that Jerry's heart has never really left Omaha. Gittel ends their affair, and Jerry decides to return to Omaha and his wife. Jerry calls to say goodbye and finally tells Gittel the words she's longed to hear from him: "I love you."

REVIEWS:

I have only admiration and respect for Shirley

Dance enthusiast and Bohemian Shirley's Gittel Mosca improvises in an old dance-studio loft.

Separated from his wife, the lonely Mitchum takes up with MacLaine as the mismatched pair moves toward deeper romance.

Though it breaks her heart, Shirley advises Mitchum to return home to Omaha and his wife.

MacLaine, but to put it bluntly she is not the Gittel I once knew and loved. . . . Given a slight Bronx veneer in the movie, she emerges as adorable and a darling, but her Hollywood background keeps peeping through.

Saturday Review

Warm and deeply felt as Shirley MacLaine's performance is, too much has been asked of her. Too much of what on stage was so surprisingly right has disappeared because Miss MacLaine doesn't have the Bronx accent and frame of mind in which this work can thrive. . . . She plays her role as a charming kook, but you know her charm comes from Texas, not from the Bronx.

New York Herald Tribune

Miss MacLaine's performance is a winning one that is sure to be talked about. Her handling of the Yiddish dialect and accompanying mannerisms is sufficiently reserved so that it does not lapse into a kind of git-gat glitterless caricature.

Variety

Mr. Wise has inevitably guided his team away from a balancing act and loaded most of the weight on Mr. Mitchum, and most of the lightness on Miss MacLaine.

New York Times

MacLaine turns on her talent like a spigot, and out comes a cooler flow of charm and humor.

Time

Shirley MacLaine has some success as the Jewish Gittel.

New Republic

NOTES:

This film was based on William Gibson's two-character play, which opened at the Booth Theatre on Broadway on January 16, 1958. It was produced by Fred Coe and directed by Arthur Penn, and it starred Henry Fonda and Anne Bancroft.

Besides suffering from all other comparisons to the stage play, critics and knowing public alike agreed the two major roles were miscast.

It can be said that this film opened new space for a more mature confrontation of the problems of young divorced women groping their way through the lonely single life in a big city.

Mitchum calls to say he's returning to his wife and will not marry MacLaine but finally admits: "I love you."

Policeman Jack Lemmon's first encounter with Shirley.

Irma la Douce

United Artists / 1963

CREDITS:

Producer, Billy Wilder; associate producers, I. A. L. Diamond, Doane Harrison; director, Billy Wilder; based on the play by Alexandre Breffort; screenplay, Billy Wilder, I. A. L. Diamond; assistant director, Hal Polaire; art director, Alexander Trauner; music, Andre Previn (score for original stage play by Marguerite Monnot); special effects, Milton Rice; cinematographer, Joseph LaShelle; editor, Daniel Mandel. Running time: 147 minutes. Technicolor. Panavision.

CAST:

Jack Lemmon (*Nestor*); Shirley MacLaine (*Irma la Douce*); Lou Jacobi (*Moustache*); Bruce Yarnell (*Hippolyte*); Herschel Bernardi (*Lefevre*); Hope Holiday (*Lolita*); Joan Shawlee (*Amazon Annie*); Grace Lee Whitney (*Kiki the Cossack*); Tura Satana (*Suzette Wong*); Harriet Young (*Mimi the Mau Mau*); Paul Dubov (*André*); Howard McNear (*concierge*); Cliff Osmond (*police sergeant*); Diki Lerner (*Fojo*); Herb Jones (*Casablanca Charlie*); Ruth and Jane Earl (*Zebra twins*); Lou Krugman, John Alavin (*customers*); James Brown (*Texas customer*); Bill Bixby (*tattooed sailor*); Susan Woods (*poule with balcony*); Sheryl Deauville (*Carmen*); Billy Beck

Shirley MacLaine as the successful Parisian prostitute Irma la Douce, plying her trade in Les Halles.

(Officer Dupont); Jack Sahakian *(Jack);* Don Diamond *(man with samples)*; Edgar Barrier *(General Lafayette)*; Richard Peel *(Englishman)*; Joe Palma *(prison guard)*.

SYNOPSIS:

Irma la Douce is a successful Parisian *poule* who plies her trade on a little street off Les Halles. She gives all her earnings to Hippolyte, her pimp. Transferred from guarding a playground to her street is young, naïve, honest, bumbling policeman, Nestor Patou.

Shocked by the open vice, Nestor conducts an unauthorized raid and arrests all the girls who frequent the bistro called Chez Moustache. Unfortunately, police Inspector LeFevre is among those arrested, and Nestor is quickly fired from the police force. Nestor takes up with Irma and,

Shirley gives the boot to Lolita (Hope Holiday), who has insulted her in front of Lou Jacobi and Jack Lemmon.

Shirley in her first meeting with the very wealthy but mysterious Lord X, played by Jack Lemmon.

after a battle with Hippolyte, becomes her new pimp. He soon falls in love with Irma and becomes jealous of her customers.

With the aid of Moustache, Nestor poses as an Englishman, Lord X, who claims he wants only a companion since a war injury has rendered him impotent. He agrees to pay Irma a huge sum for one visit a week.

But in order to pay for his disguised weekly visits, Nestor is forced to work in the produce

Shirley proudly displays her big earnings from Lord X to her pimp-lover Lemmon, as Lou Jacobi and Harriet Young look on.

Shirley and Billy Beack watch as Herschel Benardi arrests Jack Lemmon for the murder of Lord X.

market. Each morning he returns to Irma too weary to make love, and she begins to suspect he has another woman. Irma then asks Lord X to take her to England and manages to seduce the supposedly impotent Lord X.

As Irma readies to leave, Nestor decides to "murder" Lord X and dump his remains in the Seine. He is followed by Hippolyte, who, hearing a splash and seeing Lord X's clothes floating on the water, turns Nestor in as a murderer.

Nestor is sent to prison but soon learns that Irma is pregnant and escapes. He then re-emerges from the Seine as Lord X, thus vindicating himself. The moment their marriage ceremony is complete, Irma collapses and has her baby in church. Nestor is reinstated by Inspector LeFevre, and he and Irma now contemplate a blissful future.

REVIEWS:

Miss MacLaine has a wondrously casual and candid air that sweeps indignation before it and leaves one sweetly enamored of her. Though the film is less hers than Mr. Lemmon's, she is cheerful, impudent and droll.

New York Times

As to Miss MacLaine, she is a chic and piquant poule at first glance. But she is so very sweet of face that she remains virginal in all but dialogue, a sort of Sarah Lawrence girl on a sociology field trip to Pigalle.

New York Herald Tribune

It should be said that since both Lemmon and Miss MacLaine are skillful, amusing performers they bring considerable life to the movie.

Saturday Review

Miss MacLaine delivers a winning performance and has never looked better.

Variety

Shirley MacLaine is an adorable golliwog in green lingerie and inky wig; her flamboyant self-assurance is the perfect foil for the bumbling Lemmon.

Time

Lemmon marries MacLaine moments before she gives birth to their child in the church.

NOTES:

The original source for the story came from Frenchman Alexandre Breffort. The play first opened in Paris on November 10, 1956.

On September 29, 1960, it opened on Broadway at the Plymouth Theatre. It was produced by David Merrick in association with Donald Albery and H. M. Tennent Ltd. Peter Brook was the director, and Oona White did the choreography. Elizabeth Seal, Keith Michell, and Clive Revill created the roles played in the film by MacLaine, Lemmon, and Jacobi. In bringing the show to the screen, director Wilder cut the musical numbers, and the score is used merely for background.

Irma la Douce grossed more than twelve million dollars in domestic net rentals. Shirley received her third Academy Award nomination for Best Actress, this time losing to Patricia Neal for *Hud*. Shirley was named by *Film Daily* as Best Actress of the Year. She also won a Golden Globe Award from the Foreign Press Association.

The rue Casanova set was designed by Alexander Trauner to allow complete 360-degree filming. This was the first such set of its kind that permitted shooting in any direction.

Elizabeth Taylor had originally been set for the role of Irma, and Charles Laughton was to play Moustache, the philosophizing bistro owner. Laughton died, and Wilder decided he had liked the chemistry between Lemmon and MacLaine in *The Apartment* so much that he would love working with them again.

Andre Previn won an Academy Award for his Music Scoring—adaptation and treatment.

Shirley in wild getup from one of the many lavish sequences in this story of a multimillionaire woman.

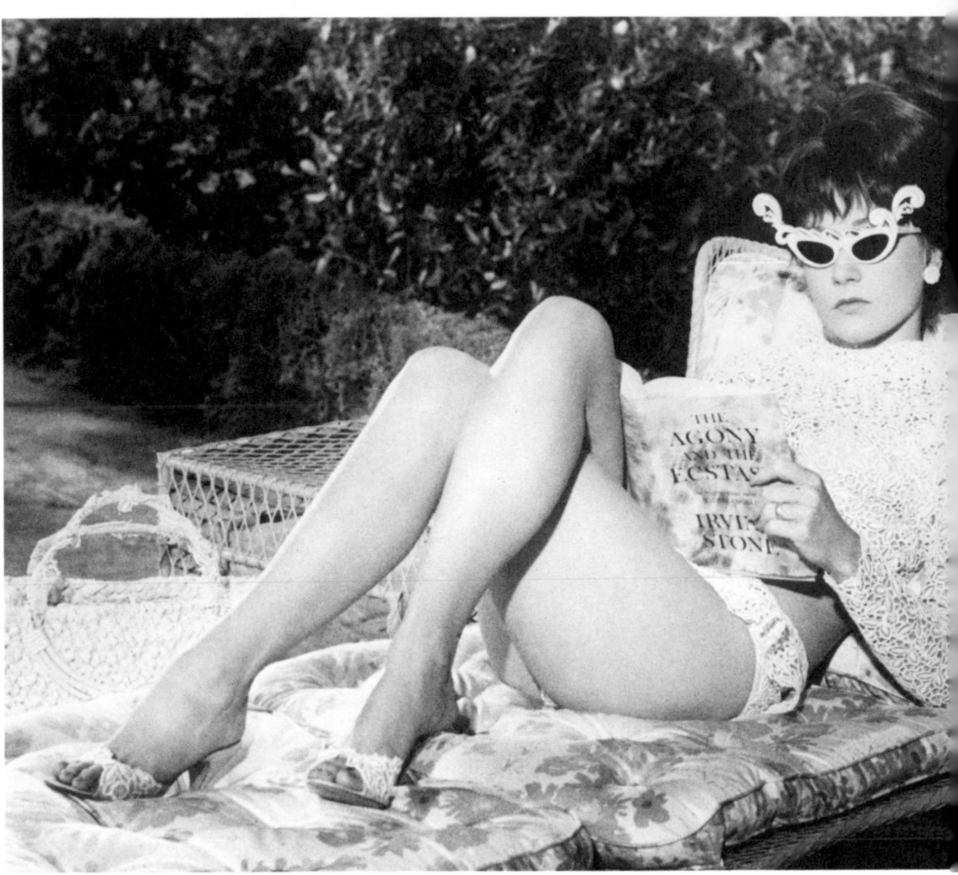

What a Way to Go

20th Century-Fox / 1964

CREDITS:

Producer, Arthur P. Jacobs; director, J. Lee Thompson; based on a story by Gwen Davis; screenplay, Betty Comden, Adolph Green; art direction, Jack Martin Smith, Ted Hayworth; music, Nelson Riddle; songs, Betty Comden, Adolph Green, Jule Styne; choreography, Gene Kelly; assistant director, Fred R. Simpson; cinematographer, Leon Shamroy; editor, Majorie Fowler; costumes, Edith Head; makeup, Ben Nye. Running time: 111 minutes. Color. CinemaScope.

CAST:

Shirley MacLaine (*Louisa*); Paul Newman (*Larry Flint*); Robert Mitchum (*Rod Anderson*); Dean Martin (*Leonard Crawley*); Gene Kelly (*Jerry Benson*); Bob Cummings (*Dr. Steffanson*); Dick Van Dyke (*Edgar Hopper*); Reginald Gardner (*Painter*); Margaret Dumont (*Mrs. Foster*); Lou Nova (*Trentino*); Fifi d'Orsay (*Baroness*); Maurice Marsac (*René*); Wally Vernon (*agent*); Jane Wald (*Polly*); Lenny Kent (*Hollywood lawyer*).

SYNOPSIS:

Louisa Benson offers the U.S. Internal Revenue Service all her wealth in a check for more than two hundred million dollars, but her offer is refused. The distressed Louisa consults psychiatrist Victor Stephanson and tells him the story of her life, in which every man she married died shortly after the wedding.

Rebelling against her money-hungry mother, Louisa, who wanted a simple life, rejected Leonard Crawley, her hometown's richest boy, to marry Edgar Hopper, a happy-go-lucky storekeeper with little interest in money. Their marriage was happy until Leonard ridiculed the barren manner in which Edgar supported his wife. Stung, Edgar became an extraordinarily successful merchant—ruining Crawley in the process—and literally worked himself to death, leaving Louisa a rich young widow.

Next, Louisa went to Paris, where she met and wed cab driver Larry Flint, who was also an unsuccessful modern artist and inventor of a machine that converted sounds into oil paintings. Everything went fine till Louisa fed classical music into the machine, resulting in a very successful painting. By building more machines and using music, Larry became enormously rich until he was entangled in his machines and killed, leaving Louisa an even wealthier widow.

When Van Dyke passes away, Shirley goes to Paris and weds a soon-to-be-successful abstract painter, Paul Newman.

Shirley rejects the town's wealthiest man, Dean Martin, to marry the poorest storekeeper, Dick Van Dyke.

Millionaire industrialist Rod Anderson was Louisa's next husband. Rod was killed by an angry bull he mistakenly tried to milk.

Song-and-dance man Jerry Pinky Benson became Louisa's number four. He became a movie star, only to be trampled to death by adoring fans at a premiere.

As Louisa finishes her story, the Internal Revenue Service calls Dr. Stephanson to tell him Louisa's check is good, and he, having thought her wealth a fantasy, faints, A janitor meanders in as Louisa is trying to revive Dr. Stephanson, and he turns out to be Crawley, her first flame, who has never regained his wealth.

After Newman succumbs, Shirley weds super-rich Robert Mitchum, who shortly thereafter goes to meet his maker.

Louisa marries him and they go live on a rundown farm where they are terribly poor until a hole in their field threatens their bliss when it begins to spout oil. To their lasting relief, they discover it's only a break in their oil pipeline.

REVIEWS:

As for Miss MacLaine and her performance, they are both not quite up to snuff. She herself seems particularly sallow, and her performance is showy but dull.

New York Times

Shirley MacLaine is the opiate of a large segment of the masses—and *What a Way to Go!* offers these addicts mainlining unlimited. For the rest of us—aware and even responsive to the charms and talents of Miss MacLaine though conscious that their variety is not infinite—this is a great big lavish star-studded box-office-oriented comedy.

New York Herald Tribune

Shirley MacLaine is a girl who can go for miles just paddling her own canoe.

Time

Being on so much of the time, Miss MacLaine obviously has the toughest assignment, and while she is always appealing, there are indications that

Gene Kelley is next, as a song-and-dance man who becomes a movie star after marrying Shirley.

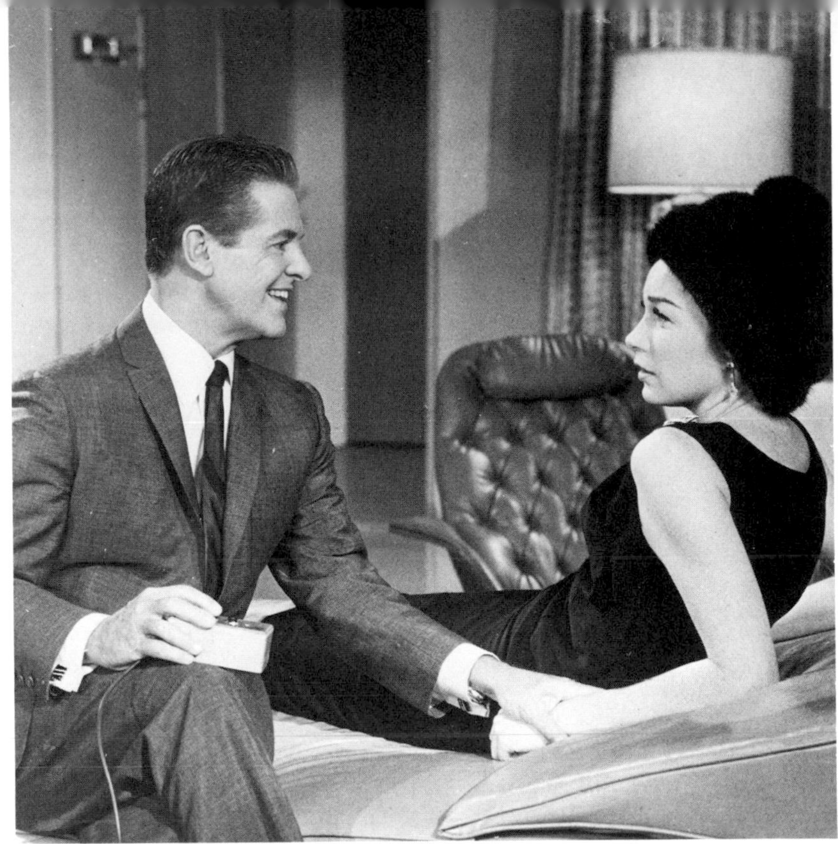

Shirley has revealed all her tales of woe to psychiatrist Bob Cummings via hypnotic flashback. Here, he wakes her at session's end.

Shortly after this dance sequence, husband number four meets his fate when he is trampled by adoring fans.

she needs the supervision of a director with a dominating talent for comedy.

Variety

Shirley MacLaine again proves that she is a stunning dancer and a stilted actress.

New Republic

Miss MacLaine is delightfully zany.

New York Journal American

NOTES:

Academy Award–winning costume designer Edith Head was allotted a five-hundred-thousand-dollar budget for MacLaine's seventy-two gowns, and Sydney Guilaroff created seventy-two different hairstyles to complement the gowns. A three-and-a-half-million-dollar gem collection was loaned to the production by Harry Winston, Inc., of New York City.

By 1964, Shirley's career had reached its zenith, in the terms Hollywood understood best. She was listed as one of the top ten box-office stars of the year and was now making eight hundred thousand dollars per film. In her position as number six after Doris Day, Jack Lemmon, Rock Hudson, John Wayne, and Cary Grant, she asked for and got a deferred percentage of the profits on her films.

This disastrous, over-opulent piece of concrete sank quickly at the box office, although Fox tried to save it via some gimmicks. The movie had a special premiere at the Better Living Pavillion at the 1964 New York World's Fair, and Fox provided a special subway train to speed press and stars and hangers-on out to the fairgrounds.

The *New York Times* estimation of Shirley's performance is certainly apt for the movie as a whole: "showy but dull."

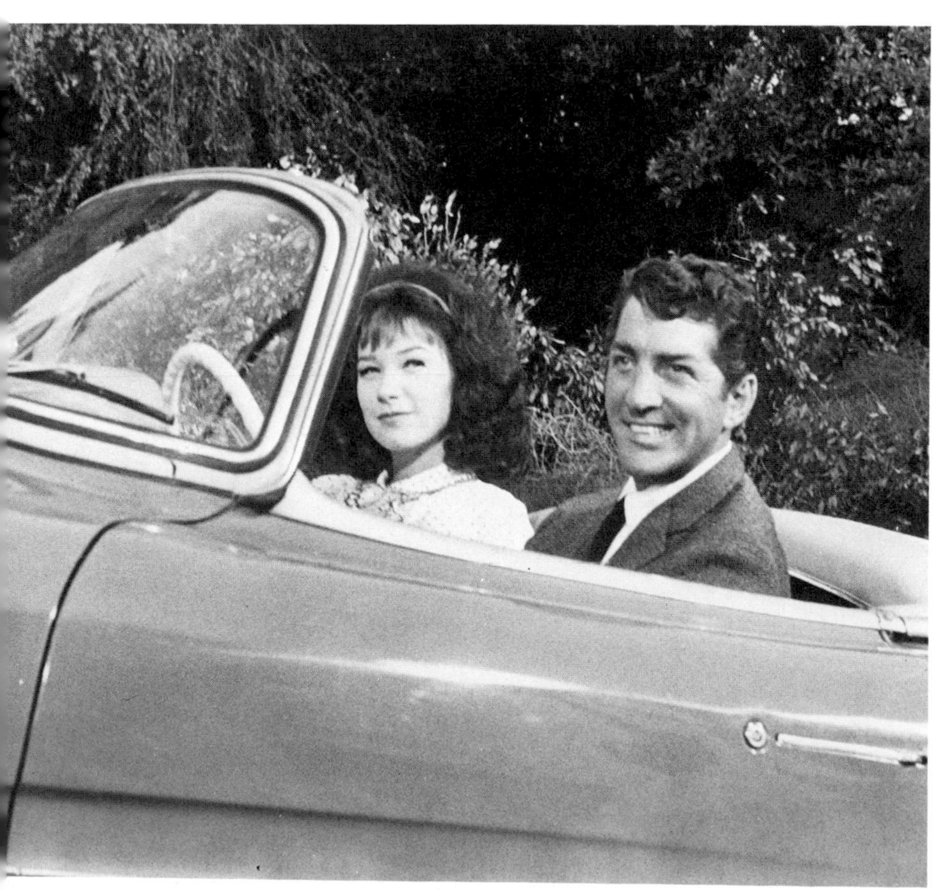

Shirley marries the once-wealthy Martin, and they go off to live in penniless bliss.

Shirley begs Crenna to pick her as his personal harem girl, which he does, thus saving her from the clutches of Fawz.

John Goldfarb, Please Come Home

20th Century-Fox / 1964

CREDITS:

Producer, Steve Parker: director, J. Lee Thompson; story-screenplay, William Peter Blatty; music, Johnny Williams; assistant director, John Flynn; choreography, Paul Godkin; cinematography, Leon Shamroy; editor, William B. Murphy. Running time: 96 minutes. Color. CinemaScope.

CAST:

Shirley MacLaine (*Jenny Ericson*); Peter Ustinov (*King Fawz*); Richard Crenna (*John Goldfarb*); Scott Brady (*Sakalakis*); Jim Backus (*Miles Whitepaper*); Jerome Cowan (*Mr. Brinkley*); Charles Lane (*editor,* Strife *magazine*); Wilfrid Hyde-White (*Guz*); Harry Morgan (*Deems Sarajevo*); David Lewis (*Subtile Cronkite*); Fred

Shirley, as the reluctant harem girl, serves up a meal for King Fawz and visiting dignitaries, as other harem girls dance.

Clark (*Heinous Overreach*); Telly Savalas (*harem recruiter*); Richard Deacon (*Maginot*); Angela Douglas (*Mandy*); Leon Askin (*Samir*); Pat Adiarte (*Prince Ammud*); Richard Wilson (*Frobish*); Milton Frome (*air force general*); Jerome Orbach (*Pinkerton*); Jackie Coogan (*Father Ryan*); Nai Bonet, Sultana (*specialty dancers*); Barbara Bouchet (*Astrid Proche*); Anne Morrell (*floating harem girl*); Irene Tsu, Shelby Grant, Eve Bruce, Gari Hardy, Jayne Wald (*harem girls*); Linda Foster (*girl*).

SYNOPSIS:

CIA Chief Heinous Overreach sends pilot John Goldfarb on a U-2 flight over the Soviet Union, in opposition to Secretary of Defense Maginot, who points out that "Wrong-Way" Goldfarb once ran a touchdown in the wrong direction in a college football game. Jenny Ericson, a *Strife*-magazine reporter-photographer, is headed for Fawzia, an Arab kingdom, where she plans to smuggle herself into the harem of the wealthy King Fawz in order to write a story about him.

Strife magazine reporter Shirley MacLaine smuggles herself into the harem of Arabian King Fawz to do a story on him.

Shirley the cheerleader and Richard Crenna the coach beg their Fawz University football team to do the impossible and win.

Fawz is furious because his son, Prince Ammud, has returned from Notre Dame with word that he did not make the football team. The King orders a football field built for Ammud and suspends relations with the United States, thus upsetting U.S. plans to build a military base in Fawzia.

Flying toward the U.S.S.R. Goldfarb is forced by mechanical problems to crash-land in Fawzia. Fawz recognizes him as the football star and gives him the choice of being turned over to the Soviets as a spy or coaching the Fawz University football team.

When Goldfarb's duties as coach begin depressing him, Fawz offers him the pick of his harem. Jenny implores him to choose her to save her from the clutches of Fawz. Goldfarb and Jenny reveal their identities to each other and fall in love.

Fawz tells Ambassador Brinkley that the United States can have its base if it will send a team to play Fawz U. America dispatches the Notre Dame team with instructions to lose, but Notre Dame refuses. In the game's final moments, however, Jenny carries the ball, and because the gentlemanly Americans will not tackle her, Fawz U. wins the game.

REVIEWS:

Miss MacLaine (who looks like a broomstick next to those luscious harem girls) appears to be mystified by the fine points of farce.

New York Herald Tribune

It might be more charitable not to mention the participants, but Miss MacLaine rates a special notation for ineptness, because her husband, Steve Parker, produced this thing. Not only is she witless but she dares expose a knobby frame in the company of a bevy of females who put her painfully in the shade.

New York Times

The name of Shirley MacLaine is about the only ingredient to keep afloat this attempt at zany comedy that mostly doesn't come off.

Variety

NOTES:

This four-million-dollar bomb was co-produced by Shirley and Steve Parker. Had it not been for the lawsuit drawn against 20th Century-Fox by Notre Dame University, *Goldfarb* would have died a swift, merciful death at the box office. The controversy and ensuing publicity drove audiences, mostly out of curiosity, to see what the great college found so offensive. What they found was Shirley at her artistic low point.

A joyful King Fawz kisses the football with which Shirley has just made a touchdown, bringing victory to Fawz University over Notre Dame. Richard Crenna congratulates Shirley.

Shirley MacLaine portrays Mae Jenkins, moll of gangster George C. Scott. Here she uses the car telephone of the fabulous Rolls-Royce.

The Yellow Rolls-Royce

Metro-Goldwyn-Mayer / 1965

CREDITS:

Producer, Anatole de Grunwald; associate producer, Roy Parkinson; director, Anthony Asquith; screenplay, Terence Rattigan; assistant director, Kip Gowans; art direction, Elliott E. Scott, William Kellner; music, Riz Ortolani; cinematographer, Jack Hildyard; editor, Frank Clarke. Running time: 122 minutes.

CAST:

Shirley MacLaine *(Mae Jenkins)*; George C. Scott *(Paolo Maltese)*; Alain Delon *(Stefano)*; Art Carney *(Joey)*; Rex Harrison *(Marquess of Frinton);* Jeanne Moreau *(Marchioness of Frinton)*; Edmund Purdom *(John Fane)*; Moira Lister *(Lady St. Simeon)*; Roland Culver *(Norwood)*; Michael Hordern *(Harmsworth)*; Lance Percival *(his assistant)*; Harold Scott *(Taylor)*; Gregoire Aslan *(Albanian ambassador)*; Isa Miranda *(Duchess d'Angouleme)*; Richard Perason *(chauffeur)*; Riccardo Garrone *(Bomba)*; Ingrid Bergman *(Mrs. Gerda Millett)*; Omar Sharif *(Davich)*; Joyce Grenfell *(Miss Hortense Astor)*; Wally Cox *(Ferguson)*; Guy Deghy *(Mayor)*; Carlo Groccolo *(chauffeur)*; Martin Miller *(waiter)*; Andrea Malandrinos *(hotel manager)*; Richard Vernon, Reginald Beckwith, Tom Gill, Dermot Kelly.

SYNOPSIS:

Three episodes are tied together by successive ownership of a superb yellow Rolls-Royce, which figures prominently in all the stories. In episode 2 we encounter Shirley MacLaine portraying Mae Jenkins, girlfriend to Mafia big-

George C. Scott tells Shirley that he must return to America on business and she must remain in Italy with Scott's henchman Art Carney.

As Art Carney and Shirley laze by the beach, along comes Alain Delon, who plays a young Italian photographer.

timer Paolo Maltese (George C. Scott), who are touring Italy together with Paolo's henchman Joey (Art Carney). Enroute they encounter Stefano, a handsome young photographer (Alain Delon). When Paolo notices Stefano's attraction to Mae, he quickly sends him away.

Paolo soon finds himself dispatched to America to liquidate a Mafia upstart, leaving Mae behind in the care of Joey. Once more, Mae encounters Stefano, and a romance soon blossoms under the watchful but tolerant eye of Joey.

When Paolo returns, it is Joey who saves Mae and Stefano from his wrath by convincing Mae to give up Stefano and return to Paolo. She pretends to Stefano that she no longer loves him and dismisses him, thus saving his life from the hands of jealous Paolo. She then returns to the side of Maltese.

Shirley has told Delon that she loves him because he has been good to her, but both must face up to the impossibility of their romance.

REVIEW:

Miss MacLaine is brash and occasionally sad.
New York Times

NOTES:

It was rather impossible for this opulent film, top-heavy with international stars, *not* to make money at the box office. Lavishly mounted and shot entirely abroad, the film was internationally successful. Shirley received third billing. This was the last film directed by the respected Britisher Anthony Asquith, who died in 1968.

Shirley's episode was conspicuous mainly because it marked the screen debut of three-time Emmy Award winner Art Carney. Said Carney: "I'd been looking for the right thing for my film debut for the last couple of years. I turned down eight pictures. Then this came through."

Alain Delon took half the salary he could have had elsewhere in order to work with this cast in an American film. He protested angrily when studio censors threatened to snip his (then) hot love scenes with MacLaine. He felt his romantic scenes would make him a star in the United States. They did not, although the scenes provoked the otherwise jaded Italian film crew to applaud at the end of the MacLaine-Delon love-scene takes.

In the grotto, Delon professes his love to Shirley.

Shirley, as the luscious Eurasian Nicole Chang, meets handsome jewel thief Michael Caine, and they team up for a heist.

Gambit

Universal / 1966

CREDITS:

Producer, Leo L. Fuchs; director, Ronald Neame; screenplay, Jack Davies, Alvin Sargent; cinematographer, Clifford Stine; art direction, Alexander Golitzen, George C. Webb; set decoration, John McCarthy; editor, Alma MacRorie; music, Maurice Jarre; choreography, Paul Godkin; makeup, Bud Westmore; gowns, Jean Louis. Running time: 108 minutes. Technicolor. Techniscope.

CAST:

Shirley MacLaine *(Nicole)*; Michael Caine *(Harry)*; Herbert Lom *(Schahbandar)*; Roger C. Carmel *(Ram)*; Arnold Moss *(Abdul)*; John Abbott *(Emile)*; Richard Angarola *(Colonel Salim)*; Maurice Marsac *(hotel clerk)*; Paul Bradley *(man in café)*.

SYNOPSIS:

While working in a nightclub in Hong Kong, a ginger-haired Eurasian woman named Nicole Chang is approached by a cockney thief, Harry Dean, and a French sculptor, Emile Fournier. The two men plan to use her in their scheme to steal a priceless Chinese statuette, the LiSsu, from Middle Eastern millionaire Ahmad Shahbandar, since Nicole's appearance is remarkably similar to that of Shahbandar's late wife, whose features resembled those of the statuette.

Posing as Sir Harold and Lady Dean, Harry and Nicole travel to Shahbandar's city of Dammuz, where he lives in a hotel penthouse. Although Shahbandar is immediately taken by Nicole, he quickly suspects their true purpose and substitutes a copy for the real statuette.

By chance, Harry discovers the hiding place

of the real statuette and removes the work, but Nicole is apprehended and told to inform him that unless the LiSsu is returned he will be killed.

Harry explains to Nicole that Emile is so accomplished at duplicating art treasures that even art dealers cannot distinguish between his work and an original. After assuring Shahbandar by telegram that the real statuette remains within the penthouse, Harry makes plans to sell a copy made by Emile two years earlier, revealing that the "theft" was a hoax designed to facilitate the sale of the fraud.

Nicole refuses to stay with Harry, however, unless he gives up his life of crime, and Harry, in a grand display of love, smashes Emile's copy

The first quarter of the film has no dialogue. Here Shirley and Caine head for a plane that is to take them to the Middle East.

Shirley in the brief attire she wears for the nightclub scene.

Shirley in one of the many hair styles and costumes worn for her role as the Eurasian.

of the statuette. As Harry leaves with the delighted Nicole, he glances knowingly at Emile. Once alone, Emile goes to a wall closet and removes three more imitation statuettes.

REVIEWS:

Shirley MacLaine and Michael Caine make an engaging couple, and the novel twist—the gimmick, so to speak—works very well.

Saturday Review

Shirley MacLaine, wearing a wardrobe that would be the envy of a sultana, is properly stoney-faced and, later, loquacious, crafty and romantic.

New York Times

Topnotch suspense comedy-romance, expert in all departments. . . . Miss MacLaine, garbed by Jean Louis in some dreamy attire, displays her deft comedy abilities after the opening segment, in which she is stone-faced and silent.

Variety

This time out, courtesy, we suspect, of director Ronald Neame, Miss MacLaine is the Shirley we fell for way back, a deft and subtle comedienne and a thoroughly charming and warmly appealing young woman.

New York World-Journal-Tribune

NOTES:

Most unique about *Gambit* is the opening dream sequence shot without dialogue at the suggestion of Shirley. The original opening of the film did not work well, so the producers tried Shirley's idea, which ended up working rather cleverly. Shirley once again received top billing in this film, which could secretly be called a mild ripoff of *Topkapi*.

Caine and MacLaine well on their way to heisting a priceless Chinese statue, the object of all their careful planning.

At the funeral of her late husband, in "Funeral Procession," Shirley is comforted by her companion Jean, played by Peter Sellers.

Woman Times Seven

Embassy-20th Century-Fox / 1967

CREDITS:

Executive producer, Joseph E. Levine; producer, Arthur Cohn; director, Vittorio De Sica; screenplay, Cesare Zavattini; art direction, Bernard Evein; cinematographer, Christian Matras; set decoration, Georges Glon; music, Riz Ortolani; editors, Teddy Darvas, Victoria Mercanton; costumes, Marcel Escoffier, makeup, Alberto De Rossi, Georges Bouban; hair styles, Alex Archambault. Running time: 99 minutes. Color by Pathé. (Filmed in Paris.)

CAST:

1. "Funeral Procession": Shirley MacLaine (*Paulette*); Peter Sellers (*Jean*); Elspeth March (*Annette*).
2. "Amateur Night": Shirley MacLaine (*Maria Teresa*); Rossano Brazzi (*Giorgio*); Catherine Samie (*Jeannine*); Judith Magre (*second prostitute*).
3. "Two Against One": Shirley MacLaine (*Linda*); Vittorio Gassman (*Cenci*); Clinton Greyn (*MacCormick*).
4. "The Super-Simone": Shirley MacLaine (*Edith*); Lex Barker (*Rik*); Elsa Martinelli (*woman in market*); Robert Morley (*psychiatrist*).
5. "At the Opera": Shirley MacLaine (*Eve Minou*); Patrick Wymark (*Henri*); Adrienne Corri (*Mademoiselle Lisiere*).
6. "The Suicides": Shirley MacLaine (*Marie*); Alan Arkin (*Fred*).
7. "Snow": Shirley MacLaine (*Jeanne*); Michael

The Many Men Of MacLaine

Actress Shirley MacLaine shares her affections among seven different leading men in Joseph E. Levine's "Woman Times Seven," Embassy Pictures' new color comedy opening .... at the .... Theatre. Under the astute directorial helm of Vittorio De Sica, Shirley is courted, cajoled and caressed by such cosmopolitan cinema idols as Michael Caine, Peter Sellers, Alan Arkin, Rossano Brazzi, Vittorio Gassman, Lex Barker and Patrick Wymark. And not a Frenchman in the crowd! Anita Ekberg and Elsa Martinelli add distaff support to Miss MacLaine.

MICHAEL CAINE

PETER SELLERS

ALAN ARKIN

ROSSANO BRAZZI

VITTORIO GASSMAN

LEX BARKER

PATRICK WYMARK

WTS-PUB-5

Joseph E. Levine presents

WOMAN TIMES SEVEN

IN COLOR

A photo of the poster advertising *Woman Times Seven.*

Caine *(handsome stranger)*; Anita Ekberg *(Claudie)*; Philippe Noiret *(Viçtor)*.

SYNOPSIS:

Funeral Procession: Leading the cortege behind her late husband's coffin, a young widow is consoled by family friend Jean; and as he confesses that he loves her, the widow's grief slowly disappears. So engrossed do they become in making plans for going away together that they miss a fork in the road and veer off to the left, while the shocked mourners continue to follow the hearse to the right.

Amateur Night: Discovering her husband in bed with another woman, an outraged wife storms out of the house vowing to sleep with the first man she meets. After joining a group of prostitutes and discovering that she is unable to carry out her threat, she accepts an accommodating procurer's offer to drive her home. When the hysterical husband greets them with insults, the procurer flattens him with one punch. Seeing her husband lying in the street, the wife runs to comfort him.

Two Against One: During an international cybernetics congress, a beautiful, bored interpreter explains to two amorous delegates, an Italian and a Scotsman, that her lover cares only for her mind and soul. To illustrate her point, she brings them to her flat and reads T. S. Eliot to them while in the nude. When one of them touches her, she furiously accuses them of reverting to the Stone Age. So repentent are they that they willingly accept cruel slaps from each

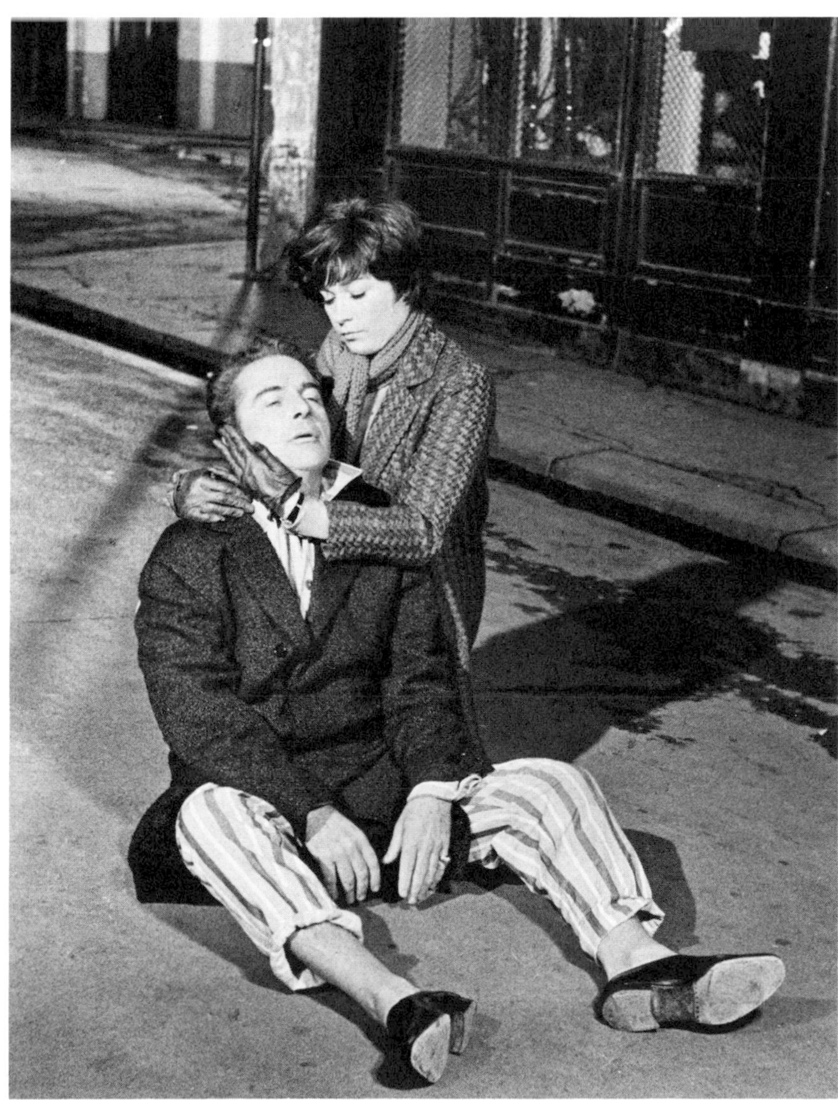

As the venegful wife, Maria Teresa, Shirley goes to the aid of her cheating husband, Rossano Brazzi, after he's been knocked out in the episode called "Amateur Night."

In the episode "Two Against One," sophisticate MacLaine meets an Italian (Vittorio Gassman) and a Scot (Clinton Greyn) at an international conference and invites them to her hotel.

In "The Super-Simone," Lex Barker (right) has called in a psychiatrist, Robert Morley, hoping he can fathom the strange pranks of Barker's wife, Shirley MacLaine, such as roller skating in the living room.

other. Greatly impressed by the demonstration, the interpreter tosses her lover's picture out the window and joins the delegates in bed.

The Super-Simone: A plain housewife is married to a hack writer known for his fictional heroine, Simone, a femme fatale who enslaves men by her wild and unpredictable nature. In a pathetic attempt to emulate the Super-Simone, the wife behaves in such a bizarre fashion that her startled husband brings home a psychiatrist. When she realizes that they believe that she has lost her mind, the wife races out of their garret apartment onto the roof and wails, "I'm not crazy. I'm just in love!"

At the Opera: When a wealthy Parisian socialite learns that a rival is wearing a copy of her new gown to the opening of the opera, she orders three of her husband's aides to bomb the rival's limousine. But a third woman, a plump and elderly matron, also appears in the same gown, and the humiliated socialite bolts out of the theater. As she does so, she spies her rival, blackened and disheveled from the bomb explosion, making a determined entrance. Anticipating her rival's reaction to the third woman, the socialite bursts into laughter.

The Suicides: Victims of a hopeless affair, a young wife and her married lover form a suicide pact. Dressed as a bride and groom, they plan to take their lives in a tacky hotel room. But they quarrel about the method they should use, and the woman sulks off to the bathroom. Once alone, the lover changes his mind and starts to sneak away. But as he opens the door he hears a window break in the bathroom. Peering out, he spots his beloved scrambling down the fire escape to the street below.

Snow: While shopping with a friend, a faithful wife discovers that they are being eyed by a handsome stranger. And when she leaves her friend, the wife is secretly thrilled to see that the man is following her. Arriving home, she greets her husband and then gazes out the window at the stranger on the street below. Overjoyed at the

Hair gorgeously coiffeured, Shirley begins to dress for an evening out in the sequence called "At the Opera."

thought that men are still intrigued by her, the wife sighs with happiness. Little does she suspect that the handsome stranger is a private detective hired by her husband to spy on her.

REVIEWS:

Despite heavy help from the makeup and wardrobe departments, [MacLaine] seldom departs from her customary screen self, and all seven women suffer from an unflattering family resemblance.

Time

. . . provides Shirley MacLaine with the opportunity to play seven different heroines in a series of vignettes directed by Vittorio De Sica. Unfortunately, since most of these females appear to be French and since Miss MacLaine appears to be firmly Americanized, she isn't always convincing.

Saturday Review

In the last episode, "Snow," husband Phillippe Noiret has wife Shirley spied upon by a handsome young stranger played by Michael Caine, whom she mistakes for a suitor.

Episodic comedy-drama, with Shirley MacLaine excellent as seven types of modern woman.

Variety

Unfortunately, Miss MacLaine is not Peter Sellers or Alec Guinness as far as versatility, let alone talent, go. It's Shirley MacLaine all the way, seven times over—and not Shirley MacLaine at her best.

NBC-TV "Today" show

All one can reasonably imagine is that Mr. De Sica and Cesare Zavattini, who wrote the script, got so completely snarled in the English language and in the American zaniness of Miss MacLaine that they lost their own Latin sense of humor and had nothing to put in its place.

New York Times

NOTES:

Though filmed in Paris, with interiors done at the Boulogne Studios, the national origin of this film is uncertain, as talents from the United States, France, and Italy are all in evidence. Though credited as a co-producer, the participation of the Societe Nouvelle des Films Cormoran is unconfirmed.

All sequences were directed on location in Europe.

In "The Suicides," Alan Arkin and Shirley play star-crossed lovers who join in a suicide pact in a tacky hotel room.

Richard Attenborough and Shirley MacLaine in one of the many delightful and hilarious sequences of the film.

The Bliss of Mrs. Blossom

Paramount / 1968

CREDITS:

Producer, Josef Shaftel; director, Joseph McGrath; screenplay, Alec Coppel, Denis Norden; cinematographer, Geoffrey Unsworth; art direction, George Lack, Bill Alexander; editor, Ralph Sheldon; music, Riz Ortolani; costumes, Jocelyn Rickards; makeup, Trevor Crole-Rees. Running time: 93 minutes. Technicolor.

CAST:

Shirley MacLaine *(Harriet Blossom)*; Richard Attenborough *(Robert Blossom)*; James Booth *(Ambrose Tuttle)*; Freddie Jones *(Detective Sergeant Dylan)*; William Rushton *(Dylan's assistant)*; Bob Monkhouse *(Dr. Taylor)*; Patricia Routledge *(Miss Reece)*; John Bluthal *(judge)*; Harry Tawb *(doctor)*; Barry Humphries *(Mr. Wainwright)*; Michael Segal *(Robert's counsel)*.

SYNOPSIS:

Robert Blossom, an overworked English brassiere manufacturer, spends his spare hours "conducting" great symphony recordings while his neglected wife, Harriet, busies herself with painting and needlework. One day Harriet's sewing machine breaks down, and Robert sends a factory worker, Ambrose Tuttle, to repair it. Upon dis-

Neglected wife Shirley busies herself painting while waiting for her harried businessman husband to come home.

A worker in her husband's brassiere factory, James Booth, comes one day to repair her sewing machine and remains four years in her attic.

covering that she shares a wildly imaginative life with Ambrose, Harriet installs him in her attic and conceals his presence from Robert.

While Scotland Yard searches for the missing factory worker, Ambrose divides his time between studying a wide variety of self-education books and re-creating with Harriet great love stories of the past. As the years pass, Ambrose's newfound talents enable him to transform the attic into a beautifully designed showplace, while Robert, driven to distraction by strange noises and by articles missing from his home, consults a psychiatrist.

The strain proves too much for Robert, and he eventually collapses and is hospitalized. Utilizing his self-taught knowledge of investments and banking, Ambrose passes stock-market tips on to Harriet, who in turn forwards them to Robert. Inevitably, Robert amasses a fortune and quickly proceeds to perfect the international brassiere.

When Robert decides to move to a home without an attic in Geneva, Ambrose sabotages a convention by arranging for Robert's inflatable brassieres to swell to such enormous proportions that the wearers float skyward.

After being forced to return home, Robert finally discovers the truth about the man who has lived in his attic for nearly four years. Announcing his intention of returning to his first love, music, Robert divorces his wife and gives Ambrose and Harriet his factory for a wedding present. Before long, it is the overworked Ambrose who leaves for work each morning, while Harriet pushes a button to summon her new lover, Robert, up from the basement.

REVIEWS:

The Bliss of Mrs. Blossom is a silly, campy, and sophisticated marital comedy, always amusing and often hilarious in impact. . . . The performances are all very good.

Variety

The picture, in lovely color, is roguish, restrained, and absurdly likeable, with a neat climactic twist.

. . . We'll buy the sly, cool impudence of Shirley MacLaine (surprisingly low-keyed).

New York Times

Much of the diversion, by the way, is supplied by Shirley MacLaine and James Booth, who sustain a note of bemused insanity throughout.

Saturday Review

NOTES:

Location scenes were filmed in London, interiors at Twickenham Studios. The source for this film was a play, *A Bird in the Nest,* by Alec Coppel. The film was released in Great Britain in December 1968, but the merging of Paramount into Gulf + Western Industries held up the distribution of this small gem of a comedy, which the *Village Voice* called "the sleeper of the year."

Poor distribution was surely a factor largely responsible for keeping this film from delighting more audiences.

Indeed, Andrew Sarris remarks in his book *Confessions of a Cultist: On the Cinema 1955/1969:* "Simply for the box-office the title should have been changed to Adultery in the Attic. . . . That's just to get the suckers into the tent. Once inside they would be treated to a bubbling, sparkling, civilized comedy of marital and extramarital manners. . . . Shirley MacLaine is the biggest revelation in the most restrained performance of her career."

Shirley divorced Attenborough to marry Booth. Now Booth is the busy husband and Attenborough has become her attic lover.

When in Southern California visit Universal Studios
"SWEET CHARITY...
Love is what it's all about!"
SWEET CHARITY · SHIRLEY MacLAINE
JOHN McMARTIN · CHITA RIVERA · PAULA KELLY · STUBBY KAYE
RICARDO MONTALBAN
SAMMY DAVIS, JR.

The original movie poster of *Sweet Charity*, with Shirley and costar John McMartin embracing.

Sweet Charity

Universal / 1969

CREDITS:

Producer, Robert Arthur; director, Bob Fosse; based on the play by Neil Simon, Cy Coleman, Dorothy Fields; adapted from the screenplay *Notti Di Cabiria* by Federico Fellini, Tullio Pinelli, Ennio Flaiano; art direction, Alexander Golitzen, George C. Webb; music, Cy Coleman; music director, Joseph Gershenson; songs, Cy Coleman, Dorothy Fields; assistant director, Douglas Green; cinematographer, Robert Surtees; editor, Stuart Gilmore. Running time: 149 minutes. Technicolor. Panavision 70.

CAST:

Shirley MacLaine *(Charity Hope Valentine)*; Sammy Davis, Jr. *(Big Daddy)*; Ricardo Montalban *(Vittorio Vitale)*; John McMartin *(Ōscar)*; Chita Rivera *(Nickie)*; Paula Kelly *(Helene)*; Stubby Kaye *(Herman)*; Barbara Bouchet *(Ursula)*; Alan Hewitt *(Nicholsby)*; Dante D'Paulo *(Charlie)*; John Wheeler *(Rhythm of Life dancer)*; John Craig *(man in Fandango Ballroom)*; Dee Carroll *(woman on tandem)*; Sharon Harvey, Charlie Brewer *(people on bridge)*; Tom Hatten *(man on tandem)*; Richard Angarola *(maitre d' at Cinematheque)*; Henry Beckman, Jeff Burton *(cops)*; Ceil Cabot *(married woman)*; Alfred Dennis *(waiter at Chili Hacienda)*; David Gold *(panhandler)*; Nolan Leary *(Manfred)*; Buddy Lewis *(appliance salesman)*; Diki Lerner *(man with dog on bridge)*;

Alma Platt *(lady with hat on bridge)*; Maudie Prickett *(nurse on bridge)*; Robert Terry *(doorman at East Fifties)*; Rogert Till *(greeter at Pompeii Club)*; Buddy Hart, Bill Harrison *(baseball players)*; Suzanne Charney *(lead frog dancer)*.

SYNOPSIS:

Charity Hope Valentine, though only a hostess in a cheap New York City dance hall called the Fandango Ballroom, refuses to be disillusioned by the disappointments life has handed her. Ever the optimist, she dreams of one day meeting the true love who will bring her happiness and respectability.

Charity's latest beau, Charlie, a gangster-gigolo, pushes her off a Central Park bridge and runs away with her life savings, leaving her with only his name tattooed across an arrow-pierced heart on her arm; nevertheless, she refuses to give up hope.

One night Charity witnesses a sidewalk argument between Italian film star Vittorio Vi-

Italian movie idol Vittorio Vitale (Ricardo Montalban) romances Charity and treats her like a lady for an evening.

Paula Kelly, Shirley, and Chita Rivera in the fabulous dance sequence atop the roof of the dance hall where they work.

After dining with Montalban, Shirley sings and dances her ecstatic wish "If My Friends Could See Me Now."

While seeking a straight job, Shirley finds herself trapped in an elevator with Oscar (John McMartin). She quickly begins a romance with the young insurance man.

tale and his elegant girlfriend, Ursula. Ursula drives off in a rage, whereupon Vittorio impulsively takes Charity to an exclusive nightclub and then back to his apartment for an intimate supper. But the evening is ruined when an apologetic Ursula arrives, and Charity is forced to spend the night hiding in one of Vittorio's closets.

Following a disastrous attempt to better herself by registering at an employment agency, Charity becomes trapped in an elevator with Oscar Lindquist, a timid, claustrophobic insurance actuary. Believing that Charity works in a bank, he asks her for a date. Despite the warnings of Helene and Nickie, her girlfriends at the Fandango, Charity decides that this romance is the one she has been waiting for all her life.

Oscar asks Charity to marry him, despite his learning that she is a dance-hall hostess; but he meets her Fandango chums at the marriage-license bureau and gets a good look at Charity's tattoo, and he is unable to go through with the wedding.

Once again, alone and abandoned, Charity wanders through Central Park until she finds herself at the bridge where Charlie deserted her. As she broods over her fate, a group of flower children hand her a daisy and thus renew her faith in what tomorrow will bring.

REVIEWS:

Miss MacLaine's sweet simplicity is so insistent that your heart strings are less tugged at than clawed at.

Newsweek

Miss MacLaine can sometimes be very comic, but she is a dull, shapeless dancer, an ordinary singer and an actress incapable of registering—outwardly—contradictory, funny internal anxieties.

New York Times

Sweet Charity is, I should think, the role which Shirley MacLaine has been building up to and waiting for all her Hollywood years. She brings off superbly the rather peculiar challenge that a musical presents: to do a singing and dancing performance which is a slice of art rather than a slice of life, yet also create a character who has some validity and identifiabilty as a creature who could exist in real life. [It] is Miss MacLaine's finest hour.

Los Angeles Times

And like the film itself, Miss MacLaine is very good, but not quite good enough. She delivers her numbers with assurance, can be cute and brassy when the occasion demands, and even shows flashes—of the first-rate musical comedy performer that she once was.

Saturday Review

Sweet Charity is a superb movie musical. It has two extraordinary performances—by Shirley MacLaine, as Charity, and Ricardo Montalban, as an Italian superstar. . . . Shirley MacLaine, as the naïve waif, gives the best performance of her career.

Newsday

Shirley MacLaine delivers her best performance ever.

Playboy

Shirley MacLaine is superb.

New York Post

NOTES:

Sweet Charity opened on Broadway at the Palace Theatre on January 29, 1966, and ran for a total of 608 performances. The producers were Robert Fryer, Lawrence Carr, and Joseph and Sylvia Harris, and the production was directed and choreographed by Bob Fosse. Gwen Verdon was Charity, Helen Gallagher was Nickie, Thelma Oliver was Helene, James Luisi was Vittorio, Arnold Soboloff was Big Daddy, and John Wheeler was Herman.

Of the original cast of featured performers, only John McMartin repeats in the film. During production of the film, Robert Arthur replaced Ross Hunter as producer, reportedly because the latter's lush production concept conflicted with Fosse's.

Location scenes were filmed in New York City. The movie was filmed in 35mm and blown up to 70mm for some roadshow presentations.

The play *Sweet Charity* was based on Federico Fellini's film *Notti di Cabiria* ("Nights of Cabiria"), released in 1957.

At the film's end, Shirley is on her own again, having lost at love once more, but she has not lost her faith in a better future.

Shirley is an unwilling shield for a would-be rapist, Armando Silvestre, as rescue arrives in the form of gunfighter Clint Eastwood.

Two Mules for Sister Sara

Universal / 1970

CREDITS:

Producers, Martin Rackin, Carroll Case; director, Don Siegel; screenplay, Albert Maltz; story, Budd Boetticher; editor, Robert F. Shugrue; cinematographer, Gabriel Figueroa; art direction, José Rodriguez Granada; music, Ennio Morricone; special effects, Frank Brendel, Leon Ortega; costumes, Helen Colvig, Carlos Chávez; stunt coordinator, Buddy Van Horn. Running time: 114 minutes. Technicolor.

CAST:

Shirley MacLaine *(Sister Sara)*; Clint Eastwood *(Hogan)*; Manolo Fabregas *(Colonel Beltran)*; Alberto Morin *(General LeClaire)*; Armando Silvestre *(first American)*; John Kelly *(second American)*; Enrique Lucero *(third American)*; David Estuardo *(Juan)*; Ada Carrasco *(Juan's mother)*; Pancho Cordova *(Juan's father)*; José Chavez *(Horacio)*.

SYNOPSIS:

While three men in the desert strip the clothes off a woman and attempt to rape her, Hogan, a gunfighter, arrives on horseback and shoots the trio to death. Hogan himself finds the disrobed victim attractive, but he is shocked to learn that she is Sister Sara, a nun involved in the Mexican revolutionary movement against the French. He agrees to take her to the revolutionaries' camp and promises to help her attack the French garrison at Chihuahua if they offer him enough money.

En route, Hogan is surprised to find Sara smoking a cigar and sneaking a drink of whiskey. Later, near the revolutionaries' camp in Santa Maria, Hogan attempts to dynamite a French ammunition train, but he is hit in the shoulder by a Yaqui Indian's arrow. After Sara bandages his wound, she climbs a high train trestle to place the dynamite and then sets off the ex-

Shirley plays Sister Sara, a nun involved in the Mexican revolution against the French.

plosion by firing a rifle bullet into the charge.

When they arrive at the rebel camp, Sara astonishes Hogan by disclosing that she is actually a prostitute with an intimate knowledge of the French fort, the revolutionaries' major military objective. They devise a plan for Hogan to take Sara to the fort as a prisoner in order to gain the confidence of the French soldiers, so that the gates will be open to the Mexicans. The plan succeeds, and the fort is captured after a bloody battle. Hogan and Sara take their share of the spoils and depart.

REVIEW:

. . . two good performances from Eastwood and Miss MacLaine. . . . Intelligence is the operative word; for although the film is also charming, funny, cruel, and sad and occasionally quite terrifying, it is by the richness and complex vigor with which it combines events, ideas, images and

Shirley points the rifle of wounded gunfighter Clint Eastwood, whose next shot will explode dynamite that will destroy a bridge.

people that it chiefly lives. . . . It is very good, and it stays and grows in the mind the way only movies of exceptional narrative intelligence do.

New York Times

NOTES:

Shot on location in Mexico, *Two Mules for Sister Sara* earned a hefty five million dollars in domestic box-office rentals. Shirley well earned her one-million-dollar fee, because the merciless Mexican sun punished her super-delicate redhead's skin all through the filming. Conditions were so bad that director Don ("Dirty Harry") Siegel hired a Mexican to accompany Shirley at all times with a giant black umbrella to shade her from the offending rays.

Eastwood stalls for time when he turns fugitive MacLaine in to French commander Alberto Morin, as part of a Juarista plot to blow up the garrison.

Production problems arose early between director Siegel and producer Rackin. Said Siegel: "Marty Rackin and I didn't get along. I'd make my points, but he would walk away saying, 'I lose the battle, but I win the war.'" The war Rackin won on *Two Mules for Sister Sara* was that "he, not I, did the final editing. It's a limited victory, because if you cut the picture in the camera, shoot the minimum . . . there isn't much leeway in editing the picture unless the producer orders more film shot." Siegel told this to Judith Kass in the book *The Hollywood Professionals*.

Shirley and Clint, shortly before he discovers that the nun he's had a hankering for is really a prostitute.

The desperate characters are upper-middle-class Otto and Sophie Bentwood, played by Shirley MacLaine and Kenneth Mars.

Desperate Characters

Paramount / 1971

CREDITS:

Producer, Frank D. Gilroy; co-producer, Paul Leaf; director, Frank D. Gilroy; based on the novel by Paula Fox; screenplay, Frank D. Gilroy; assistant directors, Norman Cohen, Francois Moullin; Music, Lee Konitz, Jim Hall, Ron Carter; cinematographer, Urs Furrer, editor, Robert Q. Lovett. Running time: 87 minutes. Color.

CAST:

Shirley MacLaine *(Sophie)*; Kenneth Mars *(Otto)*; Gerald O'Loughlin *(Charlie)*; Sada Thompson *(Claire)*; Jack Somack *(Leon)*; Chris Gampel *(Mike)*; Mary Ellen Hokanson *(Flo)*; Robert Bauer *(young man)*; Carol Kane *(young girl)*; Michael Higgins *(Francis Early)*; Michael McAloney *(raconteur)*; Wallace Rooney *(man on subway)*; Rose Gregorio *(Ruth)*; Elena Karam *(saleslady)*; Nick Smith *(caller)*; Robert Delbert *(hospital attendant)*; Shanueille Ryder *(woman doctor)*; Gonzaleo Ford *(nurse)*; Patrick McVey *(Mr. Haynes)*; L. J. Davis *(Tom)*.

SYNOPSIS:

Living in a renovated brownstone in a no-longer-fashionable block near Brooklyn Heights are Sophie and Otto Bentwood, a childless, middle-aged, upper-middle-class couple disturbed by the increasing physical and emotional violence in their urban environment. As they apathetically dine one Friday, the conservative Otto reveals that he is dissolving his law partnership with his best friend Charlie because of Charlie's newfound interest in expounding liberal causes aiding the underprivileged.

Upon hearing a stray cat scratching at the back door, Sophie gives the animal some milk, only to be severely bitten on the hand. Later, at a party given by Mike, a psychiatrist, and his wife, Flo, an examination of Sophie's hand is interrupted when a vandal hurls a rock through a window. After retiring that night, Sophie so worries that the cat might be rabid that she is unable to sleep.

When Charlie angrily bangs on the front door demanding to see Otto, Sophie persuades

Though the film was quite downbeat and received mixed critical reviews, the critics were unanimous in their praise for MacLaine's superb performance.

him to join her for a nocturnal walk. Following Charlie's confession that he is no longer happy with his wife, Ruth, because she doesn't feel anything, and that he would like to be the same kind of lawyer as the idealistic Mr. Jarndyce in Dickens's *Bleak House,* Sophie confides that at the party she had seen Francis Early, a man with whom she had a six-month extramarital affair, the only time she had ever been unfaithful to Otto.

The next morning, Saturday, Otto and Sophie awaken to find a man sprawled on the sidewalk in front of their brownstone and wonder whether he is dead or just drunk. Later, Sophie take the subway into the city, accidentally runs into Ruth (who snubs her), and then keeps a luncheon engagement with her friend Claire.

Although divorced for twenty years from her husband, Leon (a college English professor racked by the fear that his students will trick him into taking LSD), Claire is so lonely that she allows him to live with her from time to time—but only on a platonic basis. This revelation so depresses Sophie that when Claire and Leon begin to bicker, she runs out of the apartment and calls Francis; but he is too preoccupied with his latest mistress to answer the telephone.

That evening, after Otto is conned out of ten dollars by a black man who claims he only wants to borrow the money for bus fare to Albany, Sophie and Otto go to the hospital and learn that unless they catch the stray cat, Sophie will have to be given rabies shots. As Sophie and Otto anxiously wait in the kitchen, the cat returns

Shirley goes to visit her friend Claire (Sada Thompson), seeking solace, only to find her friend's life in no better shape than her own.

and is trapped in a box and then driven off by Otto to the ASPCA for examination and probable disposal.

On Sunday morning, in an attempt to escape the claustrophobic oppression of city life, Sophie and Otto drive to their summer home in the country. But their high spirits are crushed when they find the home ransacked, the windows broken, and a dead bird in the bathtub. Shattered, Otto forces the weeping and unresponsive Sophie to make love to him.

After an angry confrontation with Haynes, the hostile neighbor they hired to guard their house (and whom they suspect might be responsible for the damage), they drive back to the city, Otto casually suggesting that perhaps they should adopt a child. As Otto walks up the steps to their front door, Sophie hesitates and asks, "Suppose they've been here, too?"

Not too reassuringly, Otto answers, "Not yet; come on." And Sophie follows Otto into their darkened house to await word on the possibly rabid cat.

REVIEWS:

. . . A part that is a giant stride forward for her.

New Yorker

Miss MacLaine has done herself a favor, playing Sophie with a quiet, tasteful intelligence that effectively projects the confusion of a refugee wandering through a battle zone. It should finally establish her in the public mind as an actress of real depth.

Newsweek

Shirley MacLaine achieves one of the great performances of the year. She proves that we were right when we saw her in films like *The Apartment,* to know that she really had it all, could go all the way with a serious role.

Chicago Sun-Times

Shirley MacLaine and Kenneth Mars are quite good, managing to seem both edgy and numb at the same time.

Village Voice

. . . easily the best performance of hers I've seen.

New Republic

. . . surely one of the best female performances we will see all year.

Newsday

. . . nothing but admiration for Miss MacLaine, who seems to be as sweet and appealing as a woman at the end of her rope can be.

New York Times

MacLaine and Mars examine their vandalized country house. The shattered window symbolically represents their broken marriage.

Shirley MacLaine handles her strong, interesting role triumphantly.

Cue

Shirley MacLaine is more impressive than I have ever seen her, acting with an intensity, intelligence and maturity which erases even the dimmest trace of the charming kook who came among us years ago. She is here unstarry and is occasionally unflattered by the camera and the deliberately harsh lighting, but she is also more exciting for the depth of the feeling she conveys.

Los Angeles Times

NOTES:

Frank Gilroy's attempts to secure financing for *Desperate Characters* were unsuccessful, largely because the script was considered "too intellectual" and the proposed budget was $1,200,-000. But when Shirley MacLaine read the script she immediately phoned Sir Lew Grade, her partner in producing her television series. Grade agreed to finance the production on a shoestring budget of approximately $320,000.

Filming began entirely on New York City locations in October 1970 and wrapped seven weeks later, with MacLaine working for minimum salary plus percentage. Following the premiere in New York on September 22, 1971, Paramount Pictures (one of the companies that originally turned down the project) picked up the U.S. distribution rights to all subsequent bookings.

Barbara Trentham as Joel's girlfriend, and Shirley MacLaine as his sister, await his arrival for his birthday party.

The Possession of Joel Delaney

Paramount / 1972

CREDITS:

Director, Waris Hussein; screenplay, Matt Robinson, Grimes Grice; based on a novel by Ramona Stewart; cinematographer, Arthur J. Ornitz; music, Joe Raposo; editor, John Victor Smith; art direction, Philip Rosenberg; set decorations, Edward Stewart; costumes, Frank Thompson; makeup, Saul Meth; hair styles, Ian Forest. Running time: 108 minutes. Eastman Color.

CAST:

Shirley MacLaine (*Norah Benson*); Perry King (*Joel Delaney*); Michael Hordern (*Justin Lorenz*); David Elliott (*Peter Benson*); Lisa Kohane (*Carrie Benson*); Barbara Trentham (*Sherry*); Lovelady Powell (*Erika Lorenz*); Edmundo Rivera Alvarez (*don Pedro*); Teodorina Bello (*Mrs. Pérez*); Robert Burr (*Ted Benson*).

SYNOPSIS:

Norah Benson (née Delaney) is a wealthy divorcee living on Manhattan's fashionable East Side with her two small children. Already annoyed because her younger brother Joel chooses to live in a tawdry East Village flat rather than with her. Norah becomes genuinely disturbed when Joel goes berserk and attacks the superintendent of his building but can recall nothing of the incident.

Securing his release from a hospital mental

Perry King, as the possessed Joel Delaney, seeks out his sister Shirley MacLaine and begins to torment her.

ward, Norah moves Joel in with her and persuades him to visit a psychiatrist friend, Erika Lorenz. But Joel continues his strange behavior and is communicative only when describing his friendship with a Puerto Rican youth named Tonio.

A short time later, when Norah gives her brother a birthday party, Joel ruins it by suddenly babbling in Spanish, cursing the maid, Veronica, and insulting his girlfriend, Sherry.

In the morning, Norah takes a cab ride to Spanish Harlem and urges Veronica to come back. When Veronica says she believes Joel is possessed by an evil spirit, Norah shrugs off the suggestion—until she goes to Sherry's apartment and discovers with horror that Sherry has been decapitated.

During Joel's interrogation, the police are mainly interested in hearing about Tonio, whom they suspect of perpetrating several other bizarre murders.

Still seeking an answer, Norah returns to Spanish Harlem. This time she is informed that Tonio died months ago, that his "restless spirit" is apparently trying to take possession of her brother's body, and that it can be exorcised only through witchcraft. Despite the frenzied efforts of a medium, however, the realistic séance fails—perhaps, it is hinted, because Norah is a disbeliever.

Too frightened to remain at home, Norah heeds Erika's advice and takes the children to the family beach house on Long Island. But when she enters the kitchen the next morning, she finds Erika's severed head on a shelf by the refrigerator. A few moments later, Joel appears. Now totally possessed, he speaks as Tonio, threatens Norah with a switchblade, expresses his contempt for her high-toned manners, and de-

Shirley seeks out a medium to perform a séance to exorcise the soul of the murderer that possesses her brother.

Moments before the police shoot him down, King abuses his own sister, lustily kissing her after throwing her to the floor.

grades the children, forcing the boy first to disrobe and then to eat dog food.

The ordeal finally ends with the arrival of the police, alerted by Erika's husband, Justin. Though Joel uses the children as a shield he is felled by bullets as he races down the steps to the beach. Kneeling in the sand cradling her brother in her arms, Norah seems unaware that the evil spirit of Tonio has entered her body. As she closes Joel's eyes, she snaps open his switchblade and sneers at the police maniacally.

REVIEWS:

. . . remarkably fine performance [by Shirley MacLaine].

New York Daily News

A strikingly taut performance.

Saturday Review

. . . an unusual occult thriller [with] a riveting performance [by Shirley MacLaine].

Variety

Not all of Miss MacLaine's very good depictions of a matron confused, frustrated, infuriated and terrified serve much of a purpose.

New York

With *The Possession of Joel Delaney,* Shirley MacLaine continues an exciting new phase in her career that began with *Desperate Characters.* Gone is the vulnerable, irresistible hoyden image that all those hooker-with-a-heart-of-gold parts gave her, and in its place is the sophisticated, canny woman, beautiful yet mature, that is lots closer to the real Miss MacLaine.

Los Angeles Times

NOTES:

In February 1971, after five weeks of shooting, producer Martin Poll left the filming because of squabbling with Shirley MacLlaine. "Because of artistic differences, I have sold out my share of the picture," he announced. The film cost $1,300,000 to produce, and was also picked up by Paramount Pictures for distribution.

The film utilizes a quotation ("If you believe, no explanation is necessary. If you do not believe, no explanation is possible") which is almost an exact duplication of the quotation used for Franz Werfel's *The Song of Bernadette,* in both the novel and the film version.

Left to right: Interpreter, Madame Chou En Lai, Phyllis Kronhausen, Shirley MacLaine, Ninibah Crawford Hufford.

The Other Half of the Sky: A China Memoir

(Documentary)

CREDITS:

Producer, Shirley MacLaine; directors, Shirley MacLaine, Claudia Weill; writer, Shirley MacLaine; cinematographer, Claudia Weill; editing, Aviva Slesin, Claudia Weill. Running time: 74 minutes. Color.

SYNOPSIS:

In the spring of 1973, Shirley MacLaine was approached by representatives of the People's Republic of China to head the first delegation of American women to mainland China. She was asked to put together a group of "regular American women," rather than famous ones. She arrived in China on April 19, for a three-week stay with eleven other women. They were Claudia Weill, New York TV camerawoman; Joan Weidman, a backup camerawoman from Los Angeles; Nancy Schreiber, a New York script "girl"; photographer Cabell Glickler; Rosa Marin, head of social-work studies at the university of Puerto Rico; Pat Branson of Port Arthur, Texas; Margaret Whitman of Manchester, Massachusetts; Phyllis Kronhausen, a sexologist who runs the Museum of Erotic Art in San Francisco; Ninibah Crawford, a Navajo from Fort Defiance, Arizona; Unita Blackwell, a black civil rights worker from Marysville, Mississippi; Karen Boutillier, a twelve-year-old who had campaigned for Senator George McGovern in 1972.

Said Shirley: "These girls represent a cross-section of American womanhood. One was a delegate at the convention for George Wallace,

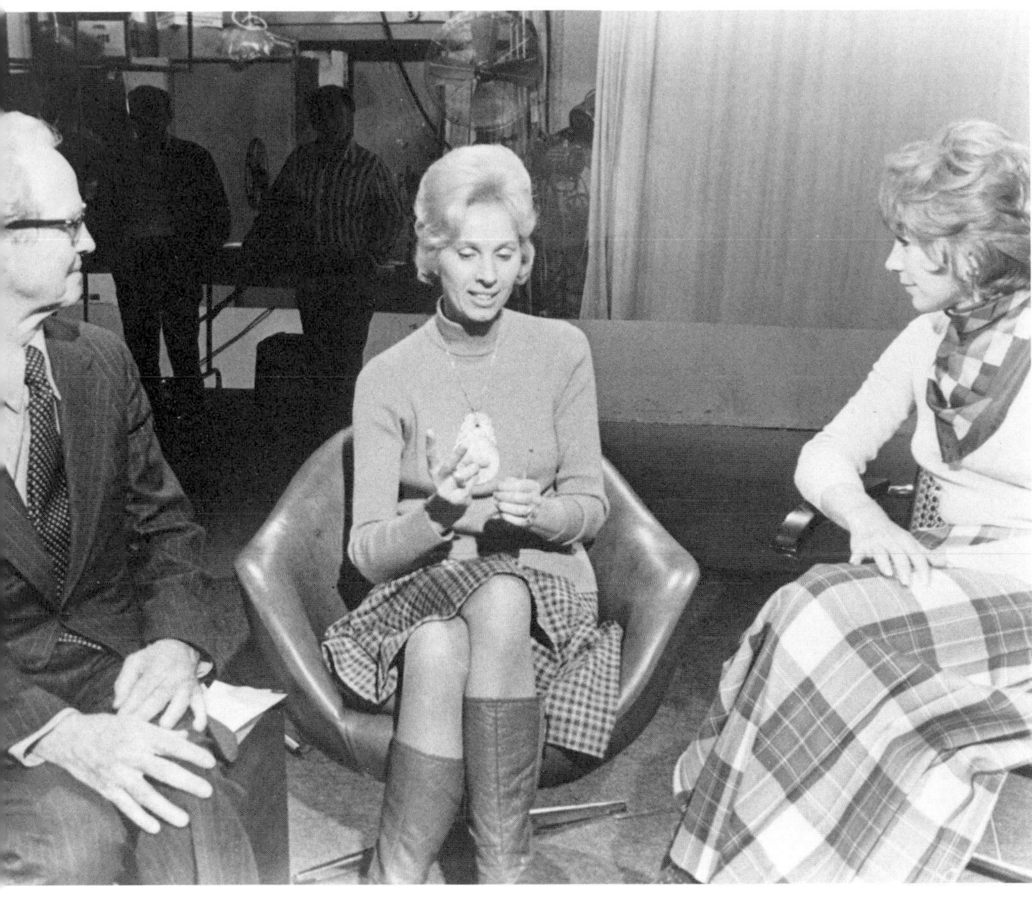

Left to right: Edmund Club, a foreign service officer in China for many years; Audrey Topping, moderator; and Shirley MacLaine discussing her film on a Public Broadcasting System program after the film's first airing on television.

An open discusson panel consisting of, left to right: Edmund Club, Audrey Topping, Margaret Whitman, Unita Blackwell Wright, Claudia Weill, Ninibah Crawford Hufford, Dr. Phyllis Kronhausen, Shirley MacLaine; backs to camera, Pat Branson, Karen Boutillier, and Rosa Marin.

one is a New England Republican conservative, one is a Ph.D.—at least, they're my idea of a cross-section."

REVIEWS:

Almost everyone is curious about China, but few will have better opportunity to experience it than those who see *The Other Half of the Sky: A Chinese Memoir.* In 1973 Shirley MacLaine visited China with a delegation of seven disparate American women and a four-woman film crew. This filmed record of what they saw is an intensely moving leap forward into a society whose values are so different from our own that China emerges as both fascinating and frightening.

Newsweek

It is the naïveté rather than the seriousness of Shirley MacLaine's *The Other Half of the Sky: A Chinese Memoir* . . . that limits the value of this documentary. . . . Most interesting, in fact, are the reactions of her "cross-sectional" American women, who, again wittingly or not, provide low comedy and sentimental relief to the aplomb and poise of all the Chinese women, including Mme. Chou En Lai.

New York

The film is astonishingly well put together, its content aided by the sharp questions put by Shirley to her Chinese hosts. What makes the film more valuable than any other visual material I've seen on today's China is Shirley's continual probing into roles and relationships, and her constant desire to understand.

Saturday Review

The Other Half of the Sky is a rough-and-ready document, filmed on the hoof during a lengthy and active tour. But it has a mighty lot to say, and says it with sincerity, humor, and uncommon charm.

Christian Science Monitor

The camera crew and other women of the American visiting group and the Chinese delegation of guides and interpreters.

As husband Tom Skerritt talks to ballet-company member Scott Douglas, Shirley takes first notice of Anne Bancroft.

The Turning Point

20th Century-Fox / 1977

CREDITS:

Producers, Herbert Ross, Arthur Laurents; director, Herbert Ross; executive producer, Nora Kaye; music, John Lanchbery; costumes, Albert Wolsky; cinematographer, Robert Surtees; editor, William Reynolds; production design, Albert Brenner; sound, Jerry Jost. Running time: 119 minutes. Color by Deluxe.

CAST:

Anne Bancroft *(Emma)*; Shirley MacLaine *(DeeDee)*; Mikhail Baryshnikov *(Yuri)*; Leslie Browne *(Emilia)*; Tom Skerritt *(Wayne)*; Martha Scott *(Adelaide)*; Antoinette Sibley *(Sevilla)*; Alexandra Danilova *(Dakharova)*; Starr Danias *(Carolyn)*; Marshall Thompson *(Carter)*; James Mitchell *(Michael)*; Scott Douglas *(Freddie)*; Daniel Levans *(Arnold)*; Jurgen Schneider *(Peter)*; Anthony Zerbe *(Rosie)*; Phillip Saunders *(Ethan)*; Lisa Lucas *(Janina)*.

SYNOPSIS:

Twenty years ago Emma and DeeDee shared the dreams of becoming great ballerinas. Today, Ballet Theatre has come to Oklahoma City, where Emma, now the principal dancer and a world-renowned ballerina, and DeeDee, now married with three children and running a local dance school, have a reunion. They are both in their forties. DeeDee now leads a middle-class life and enjoys the vicarious pleasure of watching her elder daughter, Emilia, grow to the stature of the dancer she never got the chance to be.

Emma, her life as a prima ballerina coming to an end, envies in DeeDee the family her career never allowed her to have. As they talk together their old doubts and rivalries surface. Emilia, under the sponsorship of Emma, is invited to New York for a tryout for a place in the company.

DeeDee comes to New York, to chaperone her daughter, but also to resolve the suspicions about her rivalry with Emma that have been aching for so many years. As the two women begin to face each other, each asks a silent question: Would I trade places with her?

Each woman now begins to vicariously live out her fantasies through Emilia. For Emma, Emilia is the daughter she never had, whom she can now teach and nourish. For DeeDee, Emilia's promise of becoming an outstanding ballerina

Shirley talks to her daughter Leslie Browne about the possibilities of going to New York to study ballet with Bancroft.

Leslie Browne, Shirley MacLaine, and her screen son, Phillip Saunders, walk toward Carnegie Hall.

Shirley and Anne Bancroft clown for the camera during a break in filming.

Old rivalries begin to erupt between Shirley MacLaine and Anne Bancroft as they head toward their famous fight scene.

allows her share in the world she gave up for marriage and family.

Quickly, Emilia experiences an unhappy first love affair with a womanizing young Soviet dancer, Yuri. Now readying for retirement, Emma finds her married lover is no longer willing to divorce his wife to marry her. DeeDee confronts her past in the form of Rosie, a one-time past lover, with whom she now spends a night in bed. Emilia discovers her mother's indiscretion and storms out.

DeeDee's husband, Wayne, flies to New York. DeeDee reveals to Wayne that she married him partly to prove to their peers that he was not a homosexual.

Awaiting the start of "Swan Lake," in which Emilia dances her first important role, DeeDee and Emma stroll outside the theater alone together. Their conversation quickly turns into a confrontation in which DeeDee accuses Emma of having talked her into marriage in order to remove her from the competition for a coveted role, the role that brought Emma stardom. Emma counters that DeeDee could never have been serious competition to her because she lacked the "killer" instinct that Emma possesses.

Each then furiously strikes out at the other, tearing, punching, and slapping, until they both burst into laughter and fall exhausted into each other's arms. They finally realize that each had her moment of choice—a turning point—and each has done whatever they have done. Now it is a matter of making the best of the remainder of their lives.

They return to the theater and mutually bathe in the glory that young Emilia is achieving through her marvelous dancing.

REVIEWS:

. . . Miss MacLaine and Miss Bancroft give such powerhouse performances . . .

New York Times

The performances by Bancroft and MacLaine are stunning, and both are at Academy Award level. . . . But Shirley MacLaine has had nothing so rewarding to do in such a long time and she is a terrifically effective counterpoint to

Bancroft, softer and more vulnerable yet strong enough to accept that she made the right choice.

Los Angeles Times

MacLaine's part has less razzle-dazzle, but she gives the film's most subtle, sustained performance, a penetrating portrait of a suppressed, embittered woman that risks alienating our sympathies and ends up winning them over.

Newsweek

It's enhanced by incandescent performances from Anne Bancroft and Shirley MacLaine.

Hollywood Reporter

Will rank as one of MacLaine's career highlights.

Variety

If I had to choose the performances I admired most in both *Julia* and *The Turning Point,* I would pick the work of Shirley MacLaine. MacLaine is the one you'll remember. . . . She's dead center in her portrayal of a woman who has turned a corner in life and suddenly feels lost.

Chicago Tribune

The balance would be overwhelmingly in favor of the career woman were it not for Shirley MacLaine's magnificence in the role of the Oklahoma City housewife who follows her daughter to New York for one last glimpse of the world she gave up.

New York

MacLaine, returning to the less frenetic "simplicity" that was her early-career charm, brings an honesty to her forthright emotional reactions that is completely disarming.

New York Post

NOTES:
Had she not fallen ill, Gelsey Kirkland, of the American Ballet Theatre, would have played the ingenue role played by Leslie Browne in the film. However, the film is based coincidentally on Browne's family, who twenty-five years ago left New York and the American Ballet Theatre to go west and found their own ballet school. They returned, just as in the film, when Leslie earned a scholarship to ABT.

Shirley and director Herbert Ross discuss an upcoming scene during a break in filming.

As Eve Rand, Shirley shares a tender moment with her ailing husband, financier Benjamin Rand (Melvyn Douglas).

Being There

United Artists / 1979

CREDITS:

Producer, Andrew Braunsberg; executive producer, Jack Schwartzman; associate producer, Charles Mulvehill; director, Hal Ashby; screenplay, Jerzy Kosinski, based on his novel; director of photography, Caleb Deschanel; production design, Michael Haller; costumes, May Routh; music, John Mandel; makeup, Charles Schram, Frank Westmore; editor, Don Zimmerman; art director, James Schoppe; set decorator, Robert Benton; special photography, Dianne Schroeder; casting, Lynn Stalmaster. Running time: 130 minutes. Technicolor. Color by Metro-Color.

CAST:

Peter Sellers (*Chance*); Shirley MacLaine (*Eve Rand*); Melvyn Douglas (*Benjamin Rand*); Jack Warden (*President Bobby*); Richard Dysart (*Dr. Robert Allenby*); Richard Basehart (*Vladimir Skrapinov*); Ruth Attaway (*Louise*); Dave Clennon (*Thomas Franklin*); Fran Brill (*Sally Hayes*); Denise DuBarry (*Johanna Franklin*); Oteil Burbridge (*Lolo*); Ravenell Keller III (*Abbaz*); Brian Corrigan (*policeman*); Alfredine Brown (*old woman*); Donald Jacob (*David*); Ernest M. McClure (*Jeffery*); Kenneth Patterson (*butler*); Richard Venture (*Wilson*); Arthur Grundy (*Arthur*); W. C. "Mutt" Burton (*Lewis*); Henry B. Dawkins (*Billings*); Georgine Hall (*Mrs. Aubrey*); Nell Leaman (*Constance*); Villa Mae Barkley (*Teresa*); Alice Hirson (*first lady*); James Noble (*Kaufman*); Timothy Shaner, William F. Williams, William Dance, Jim Aar, William Lubin (*presidential aides*); Gerald C. McNabb, Jr., Hoyt Clark Harris, Jr., (*secret-service agents*); Ned Wilson (*Honeycutt*); Stanley Grover (*Baldwin*); John Harkins (*Courtney*); Katherine De-

Hetre *(Kinney)*; William Larsen *(Lyman Stuart)*; Jerome Hellman *(Gary Burns)*; Arthur Rosenberg *(Morton Hull)*; Sam Weisman *(Colson)*; Fredric Lehne *(TV page)*; Gwen Humble *(TV guest)*; Laurie Jefferson *(TV reporter)*; Allen Williams, Janet Meshad, Paul Marin *(other reporters);* Melendy Britt *(Sophie)*; Hanna Hertelendy *(Natasha Skrapinov)*; Elya Baskin *(Karpatov)*; Thann Wyenn *(Ambassador Gaufridi)*; Richard McKenzie *(Ron Steigler)*; Sandy Ward *(Senator Slipshod)*; Danna Hansen *(Mrs. Slipshod)*; Mitch Kreindel *(Dennis Watson)*; Richard Seff, Terence Currier, Leon Greenberg, Austin Hay, Mark Hammer, Maurice Copeland *(pallbearers)*.

SYNOPSIS:

Being There is a comic fable about a man called Chance whose naïveté and essential innocence precipitate a series of hilarious adventures through the political labyrinth of the nation's capital.

Chance is without known parentage or background, having been cared for since childhood by an old man whose garden he lovingly tended. Unable to either read or write, he has spent his many leisure hours watching television, and only from television has he gained knowledge of life outside the house. Upon the man's demise, the house is closed, and Chance is sent away. He has only a few bewildered hours in which to discover the real world, however, before he is hit by a limousine carrying Eve Rand (Shirley MacLaine), wife of the country's most powerful financier, a man of enormous political influence

Taken to the Rand estate for medical attention, Chance magically charms everyone: Eve's dying husband, Benjamin; the president of the United States; other powerful personages; and Eve Rand herself. They see his invocation of simple garden metaphors for the country's complex economic ills as a fresh and different kind of wisdom. By the story's finale, Chance the gardener has become a celebrity and man of influence.

Thematically, *Being There* deals with the pervasive influence of television in our lives, of the ways in which the medium alters our perception of the world, and of its transforming effect on people and events. Its impact is felt perhaps most directly in the upper echelons of government; hence the story's setting of Washington.

Peter Sellers as Chauncey Gardiner and Shirley MacLaine as Eve Rand arrive at a formal party in Washington.

On a different level, *Being There* may be seen as a parable about the power of simplicity. Chance's monastic existence has left him, in the words of the director, "with a childlike aura," and in the words of the author, "devoid of any particular will which might trigger a negative reaction." People respond to him affirmatively, imbuing the simple gardener with virtues of wisdom, insight—even holiness—largely absent from others in the world around them.

REVIEWS:

There is a superb ensemble playing in "Being There." Mr. Sellers never strikes a false note. The other fine actors in "Being There"—Melvyn Douglas as a poignantly ailing rich man, Shirley MacLaine as his sexy, sprightly wife. . . . The timing is often so perfect that the film, at its very wittiest, strips conversation down to its barest maneuvers and stratagems. "Being There" is a stately, beautifully acted satire.

New York Times

In a role more difficult than it may seem, Shirley MacLaine is subtle and winning, retaining her dignity despite several precarious opportunities to lose it. . . . "Being There" is a highly unusual and unusually fine film.

Variety

Shirley MacLaine is Eve Rand, the pampered and slightly dizzy wife of the richest and most powerful man in the United States.

Sellers and his hostess, MacLaine, pay rapt attention to the political conversation at a Washington party.

MacLaine adds marvelous presence and stature to the role of [Sellers's] benefactor, whose affection gradually turns to desire. It's a glamorous characterization and MacLaine develops it most appealingly. . . . One of the most charming motion pictures of the year.

Hollywood Reporter

Shirley MacLaine is especially endearing as Eve with her frantic, but futile attempts to seduce Chance. . . . An incredibly delightful movie. . . . Marvelously wry, sharp-witted script. . . . Nurtured along by director Hal Ashby, "Being There" is so deliciously absurd that it keeps one in almost a constant state of laughter.

New York Daily News

NOTES:

Being There was filmed in Los Angeles; Washington; and Asheville, North Carolina. Certain rooms in the White House were re-created on the sound stage in L.A. Chance's meticulous garden and greenhouse were created on MGM's lot number 2. The setting for his original home was the Pasadena Historical Society, former residence of the Finnish consul general. The famed Biltmore, serving as the Rand mansion, was the film's primary location. Situated on ten thousand wooded acres in the Blue Ridge mountains of North Carolina, it was constructed between 1890 and 1895 by George Vanderbilt, grandson of the "commodore," Cornelius Vanderbilt.

It took almost eight years to get author Kosinski to relinquish rights to his story so it could be filmed. It took time to find financial backing, because many studio executives, although they were interested in the project, were reluctant to take a chance on such unusual material.

"I was captivated by the story," says Peter Sellers. "And I liked the way Hal [Ashby] dealt with humor. It's like we used to do in England on the 'Goon Show,' a kind of put-on humor, a satire done completely straight. The fun is in the situation."

Negligee-clad Shirley MacLaine relaxes after an exhausting workout trying to capture the fancy of Chance (Peter Sellers).

Shirley MacLaine on Television

Shirley greeting cameramen and crew outside her home in Royal Oaks, California. They were there to film her being interviewed by Edward R. Murrow on CBS-TV's *Person to Person,* broadcast March 6, 1959.

"I think television is infinitely more interesting than films—certainly more courageous," said a daring Shirley MacLaine.

"It's a medium for showing your imperfections. That's what people love. Women are fabulous in television. It's a woman's medium."

Nowadays Shirley limits herself to one television special per year. She told the *New York Daily News,* "I spend all the money the network gives me for the hour and I stay up until 4 in the morning trying to get it perfect. It's only once a year, but it's good when it's there. It sounds like my sex life."

Shirley's track record on television fares well when it comes to specials. Of the half dozen she's done, she won four Emmy Awards. She's a welcome guest on many variety and talk shows because she is always open, gregarious, and delightful—and never dull.

Shirley began her television career back in 1955, when she first appeared on General Foods' *The Bob Hope Show* as a guest performer. She followed that almost imediately with the appearance that made her name a household word across America. In a story that closely parallels the incident with Carol Haney in *Pajama Game,* movie star Betty Grable injured her leg, rendering her unable to perform the lead in the musical revue "That's Life" on the *Shower of Stars* television show broadcast February 17, 1955, on

Shirley and Dinah Shore as marionettes, in one of Shirley's many appearances on *The Dinah Shore Chevy Show,* during the 1957–58 season.

A publicity still from ABC-TV's *Shirley's World,* which premiered September 15, 1971.

CBS-TV. Shirley was quickly brought in to sing and dance and co-star with Harry James, Larry Storch, and Anna Maria Alberghetti. Once again, Shirley was a smash hit.

Dissatisfied with her contract with Hal Wallis, Shirley exercised the portion of that contract allowing her to make frequent appearances on television. On television she was free to be much more spontaneous and easygoing than on film. In 1958 she signed a three-year contract with NBC, agreeing to appear fifteen times for a five-hundred-thousand-dollar fee, much of which went to Hal Wallis.

In 1970, after years of appearing on talk and variety shows as a guest, Shirley was approached by the British impresario Sir (now Lord) Lew Grade, multimillionaire creative brain behind ATV-ITC British television. Grade offered Shirley a deal worth in excess of twelve million dollars to head her own television series, plus make three films for less than three million dollars.

The series, *Shirley's World,* bowed simultaneously here and in Britain on September 15, 1971, as a half-hour comedy-adventure series with Shirley MacLaine portraying Shirley Logan, a globe-trotting photo-journalist. Lavishly produced in England and all around the globe by Sheldon Leonard (of TV's *I Spy* fame), it seemed like a sure winner. At $47,500 salary per episode, Shirley was the highest-paid star in television. From the very first episode the show bombed terribly. The critics were merciless. After seventeen episodes, ABC-TV canceled on January 9, 1972, and *Shirley's World* slid off the globe.

Reflecting to the *New York Post* on the defunct series in 1978, Shirley said, "It was a mistake I made in agreeing to do it and a mistake in the way they handled it. I should have gone into TV singing and dancing. You can take the girl out of the chorus, but you can't take the chorus out of the girl."

In the beginning stages of *Shirley's World,*

both her and Grade's hopes ran high. Grade wanted her because he believed Shirley was known to every household in America. He would use her name to attract other American stars to England, work on more television projects, and ultimately raise the level of television broadcasting in America, while also making himself a power in America as he is in Britain.

Shirley envisioned a handsomely mounted, finely acted and directed program that would not pander to "the vanilla ice-cream fantasy land" to which so many other American situation comedies were reduced. Shirley saw a show that "moved people, cheered them up, made them believe in the essential humanity of themselves and others," she admitted in her book *You Can Get There from Here.*

When the first scripts arrived Shirley quickly saw they were stereotypical and tasteless. "I was playing a nosy, irritating, empty-minded little banana head, who goes around the world bother-

A portrait of Shirley depicting her as Shirley Logan, a globe-trotting photojournalist.

Shirley photographs children and plays with them in this episode shot in the Philippines.

Shirley visits with Kabuki players in Japan.

ing people. Worse, the people Shirley Logan bothered were even lower on the human scale than she was. The Italians pinched her, the Arabs stole, the Chinese were stupid and mercenary, the Japanese were buck-toothed, secretive Mr. Motos, the Irish were drunks, the Spaniards were lazy liars," Shirley revealed in *You Can Get There from Here.*

When she voiced her disappointment to Grade, he quietly replied there was easily twenty

Shirley tosses a fan during the tea ceremony in a Japanese geisha house.

million dollars riding on this show and there was absolutely no time to postpone, change, edit, revise, or redo anything.

The critics were not kind in their appraisal, calling Shirley and the show: "Dismal . . . Blundering . . . Thudding . . . Painfully disappointing show." *Variety* said: "Sheldon Leonard has placed a heavy burden on Miss MacLaine's able shoulders. As a femme version of Hildy Johnson in this Blighty update of the old *Front Page,* she's going to have to be a lot less liberated than the booze-swilling newshounds in the Hecht-MacArthur original. . . . Unless Miss MacLaine's personal life becomes more interesting in the series, 'World' is going to look repetitive."

Before and after the series, in 1968 and 1972 respectively, Shirley made noncommercial appearances on television as a delegate to the Democratic National Convention in those election years. In 1968, she was interviewed by Edwin Newman on the convention floor at al-

Shirley snaps away like the professional she portrayed in her only attempt at a television series of her own.

Shirley and a geisha friend stand before a statue of Buddha in Japan.

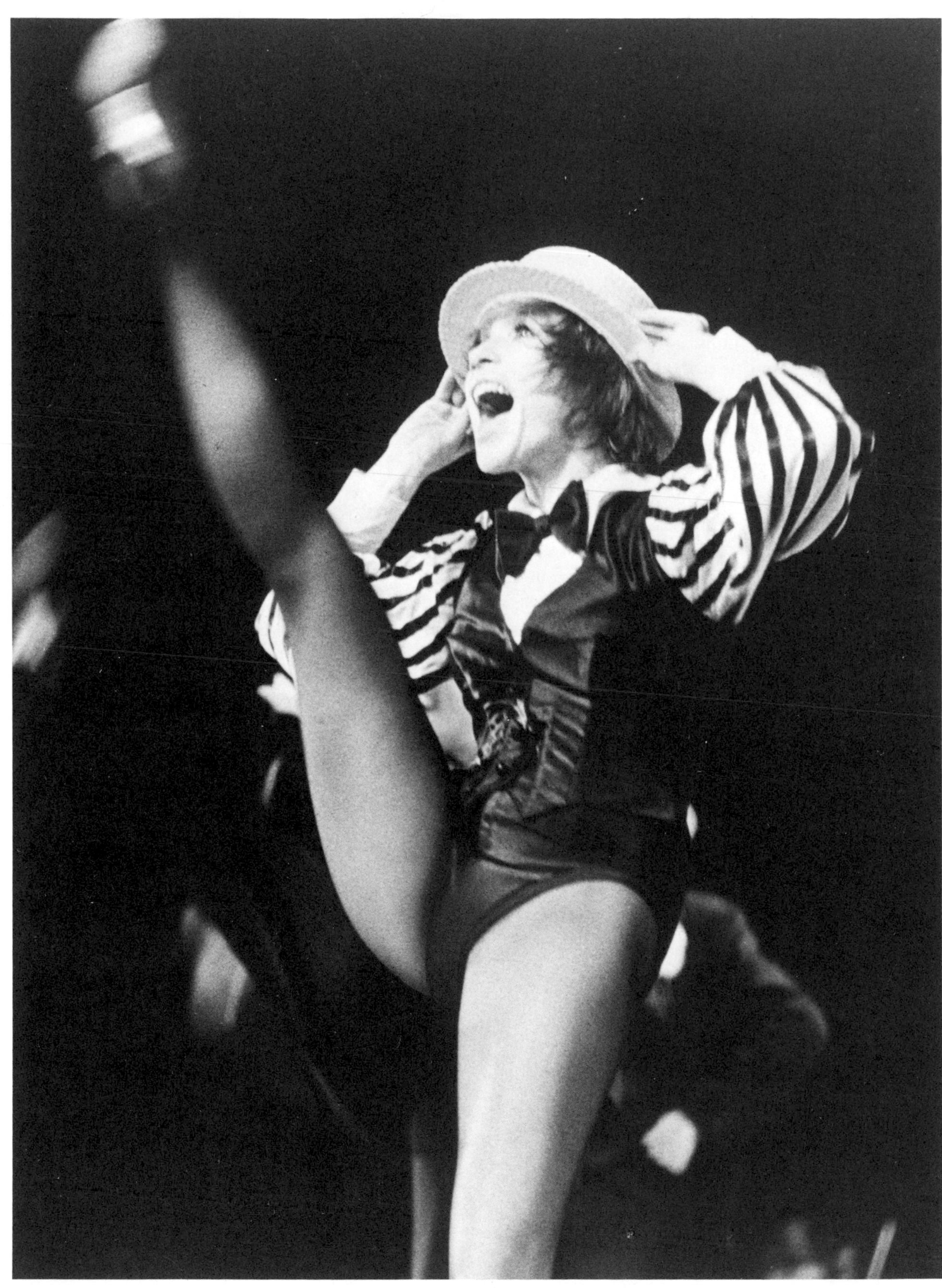

Shirley kicks high in her Emmy-winning CBS-TV Special *Gypsy in My Soul,* which aired on January 20, 1976.

Shirley and her "gypsies" give their all during this dance routine.

most 2:00 A.M. She had just signed a draft–Ted Kennedy petition, although she was still officially committed to George McGovern. In 1972, she was interviewed on the convention floor about her invitation to McGovern's hotel at the time he was about to choose a vice-presidential running mate. The interview was fascinating, because Shirley recalled suggesting a black or a woman to McGovern for the VP spot on the ticket.

Shirley trailblazed on television when, in 1975, her documentary on her trip to the People's Republic of China, which she produced and co-directed, was aired on Public Broadcasting System educational stations throughout the country and received excellent critical notices everywhere.

In the latter 1970s Shirley appeared in several very successful television specials. Her CBS-TV special "If They Could See Me Now" won three Emmy Awards. "Gypsy in My Soul," which she produced herself through MacLaine Productions, won yet another Emmy.

Of her overall experience of television, Shirley says simply: "I wanted to . . . to stretch myself, and the fact that a performer does that is in itself a communicative statement."

Following is a list of Shirley MacLaine's network television appearances:

Shirley talks about America as she sees it in this appearance in *Celebration: The American Spirit* on ABC-TV, January 25, 1976.

In NBC-TV's Special *The Big Event: "Life" Goes to the Movies,* Shirley talks about her career in films and about Hollywood.

Television Appearances of Shirley MacLaine

February 1, 1955 *The Bob Hope Show,* NBC.

February 17, 1955 *Shower of Stars,* CBS.

April 2, 1955 *Easter Seal Teleparade of Stars,* CBS.

April 6, 1955 *The Sheilah Graham Show,* NBC.

July 27, 1955 *Today* (interviewed), NBC.

December 6, 1955 *The Chevy Show Starring Ethel Merman,* NBC.

April 21, 1956 *The George Gobel Show,* NBC.

October 17, 1956 *Tonight* (interviewed briefly via microphone pickups from Rivoli Theatre, New York City, where *Around the World in 80 Days* premiered), NBC.

November 30, 1956 *The Chevy Show Starring Dinah Shore,* NBC.

December 30, 1956 *The Steve Allen Show* (interviewed on film at the Hollywood premiere of *Around the World in 80 Days),* NBC.

March 20, 1957 *It Could Be You,* NBC.

March 22, 1957 *The Chevy Show*—"The Dinah Shore Show," NBC.

June 2, 1957 *The Chevy Show*—"The Pat Boone and Shirley MacLaine Show," NBC.

November 3, 1957 *The Dinah Shore Chevy Show,* NBC.

December 8, 1957 *The Chevy Show Starring Nanette Fabray,* NBC.

January 5, 1958 *The Chevy Show Starring Tom Ewell,* NBC.

March 9, 1958 *The Dinah Shore Chevy Show,* NBC.

March 26, 1958 The Thirtieth Annual Academy Awards Oscar telecast (in entertainment portion, doing medley of songs with others), NBC.

April 15, 1958 Emmy Awards (in entertainment portion), NBC.

May 25, 1958 *The Chevy Show Starring Shirley MacLaine* (hostess and emcee), NBC.

June 8, 1958 *The Dinah Shore Chevy Show,* NBC.

November 2, 1958 *The Chevy Show Starring Sid Caesar,* NBC.

December 14, 1958 *The Dinah Shore Chevy Show*, NBC.

February 1, 1959 *The Chevy Show Starring Shirley MacLaine* (with 15 outstanding performers of Japan's television), NBC.

March 6, 1959 *Person to Person* (Edward R. Murrow interviews Shirley MacLaine, husband Steve Parker, and daughter, Stephanie Sachiko), CBS.

November 19, 1959 *The Jack Paar Show* (guested with husband, made appeal for Japanese typhoon victims), NBC.

November 24, 1959 *The Jack Paar Show,* NBC.

April 18, 1961 *Here's Hollywood,* NBC.

September 23, 1964 *Wednesday Night at the*

With the energy everpresent in all her song-and-dance performances, Shirley lets go in this moment from her CBS-TV Special *Where Do We Go from Here* broadcast March 12, 1977.

Shirley with her longtime friend and political ally former New York congresswoman Bella Abzug, as they appeared on NBC-TV's *Laugh-in*, December 20, 1977.

Movies (starred as Sharon Kensington in *Career*), NBC.

November 14, 1964 *Saturday Night at the Movies,* (starred as Ginny in *Some Came Running*), NBC.

March 15, 1966 *Tuesday Night at the Movies* (starred as Anna Vorontosov in *Two Loves*), NBC.

March 17, 1965 *Wednesday Night at the Movies* (co-starred as Virginia in *Hot Spell*), NBC.

August 26, 28, 29, 1968 Democratic National Convention (interviewed and made comments on convention proceedings), CBS.

August 26, 1968 Democratic National Convention from Chicago (interviewed on convention floor by Edwin Newman after she signed draft-Kennedy petition), NBC.

August 28, 1968 *Today* (interviewed at Democratic National Convention as delegate from California), NBC.

October 8, 1968 *Tuesday Night at the Movies* (starred as Nicole Chang in *Gambit*), NBC.

October 14, 1969 *The Tonight Show Starring Johnny Carson,* NBC.

April 19, 1970 *Prudential's On Stage Presents the Tony Awards* (co-host), NBC.

July 13, 1970 *NBC Monday Night at the Movies* (starring as Gittel Mosca in *Two for the Seesaw*), NBC.

November 19, 1970 *Today* (interviewed on her book *Don't Fall Off the Mountain*), NBC.

December 22, 1970 *A World of Love* (co-hosted this special with Bill Cosby saluting children around the world), CBS.

September 15, 1971 *Shirley's World* (starred as Shirley Logan in weekly drama-adventure series; premiere), ABC.

February 11, 1972 *NBC Friday Night at the Movies* (starred as Sister Sara in *Two Mules for Sister Sara*), NBC.

June 5, 1972 *Today* from Los Angeles (guest

Shirley appeared with Mike Douglas on his show when it was telecast from Monte Carlo in November 1977.

on behalf of Senator George McGovern and spoke on entertainers in politics), NBC.

July 11, 1972 *Election '72—Democratic National Convention* (on floor—asks for vote of conscience on the abortion minority report; predicts issue will be voted down; is against abortion plank but will vote for it—is not sure it belongs in politics), NBC.

July 13, 1972 *Election '72—Democratic National Convention* (off floor—interviewed on invitation to Senator McGovern's hotel to discuss vice-presidential selection; suggested a black or a woman for the VP spot), NBC.

January 20, 1973 *NBC Saturday Night at the Movies* (starred as Fran Kubelik in *The Apartment),* NBC.

April 20, 1973 *Today* (guest appearance), NBC.

December 29, 1973 *NBC Saturday Night at the Movies* (starring as Charity in *Sweet Charity),* NBC.

March 18, 1974 *American Film Institute Salute to James Cagney* (co-presenter of Life Achievement Award), CBS.

April 2, 1974 The 46th Annual Academy Awards, Oscar telecast (guest appearance), NBC.

November 28, 1974 *If They Could See Me Now* special (Shirley traces her career in show business in this one-hour musical autobiography; Carol Burnett is her special guest), CBS.

March 12, 1975 *Today* (guest appearance discussing her new book, *You Can Get There from Here*), NBC.

April 1, 1975 *The Tonight Show Starring Johnny Carson* (guest appearance), NBC.

April 8, 1975 The 47th Annual Academy

Shirley laughs it up with Phil Donahue on his show in Chicago in 1978.

Awards, Oscar telecast (guest appearance), NBC.

April 15, 1975 *The Other Half of the Sky: A China Memoir* (documentary produced by Shirley MacLaine), PBS.

October 4, 1975 *The Carol Burnett Show* (guest appearance), CBS.

October 24, 1975 *Texaco Presents Highlights of a Quarter Century of Bob Hope Specials* (appears in one of the segments), NBC.

January 20, 1976 *Gypsy in My Soul,* special (musical-comedy and dramatic hour celebrating the theatrical chorus, starring Shirley MacLaine; special guest star, Lucille Ball), CBS.

January 25, 1976 *Celebration: The American Spirit,* special (guest appearancc), ABC.

July 14, 1976 *Tomorrow* (guest appearance), NBC.

October 31, 1976 *The Big Event—Life Goes to the Movies* (guest appearance), NBC.

November 21, 1976 *The Big Event—NBC: The First Fifty Years* (guest appearance in segments of old NBC shows).

January 19, 1977 *Inaugural Eve Gala Per-*

Shirley enjoys herself with old friend Dinah Shore and guest Jane Wyman on the *Dinah!* show, March 8, 1978.

formance Special (special entertainment tribute to President Elect Carter and Vice-President Elect Mondale by artists in music, theater, poetry, and sports), CBS.

March 3, 1977 *Las Vegas Entertainment Awards* (guest appearance as an award recipient), NBC.

March 12, 1977 *Where Do We Go from Here* (special starring Shirley MacLaine; a musical romp through our nation's next 100 years; guest stars, Les Ballets Trocadero de Monte Carlo, Don Ellis and his Electric Orchestra, and Laserium), CBS.

August 29, 1977 *The Big Event—Life Goes to the Movies* (guest appearance), NBC.

September 11, 1977 *The Big Event: Emmy Awards* (guest appearance), NBC.

November 29, 1977 *America Salutes the Queen* (guest appearance), NBC.

December 20, 1977 *Laugh-in* (guest appearance), NBC.

January 29, 1978 35th Annual Golden Globe Awards (guest appearance, award recipient), NBC.

March 3, 1978 *The Tonight Show Starring Johnny Carson* (guest appearance), NBC.

March 22, 1978 *Today* (guest appearance), NBC.

March 26, 1978 *Second Annual Hollywood Outtakes* (guest appearance in old film segments), NBC.

April 3, 1978 *Today* (guest appearance), NBC.

Person to Person: Edward R. Murrow Interviews Shirley MacLaine

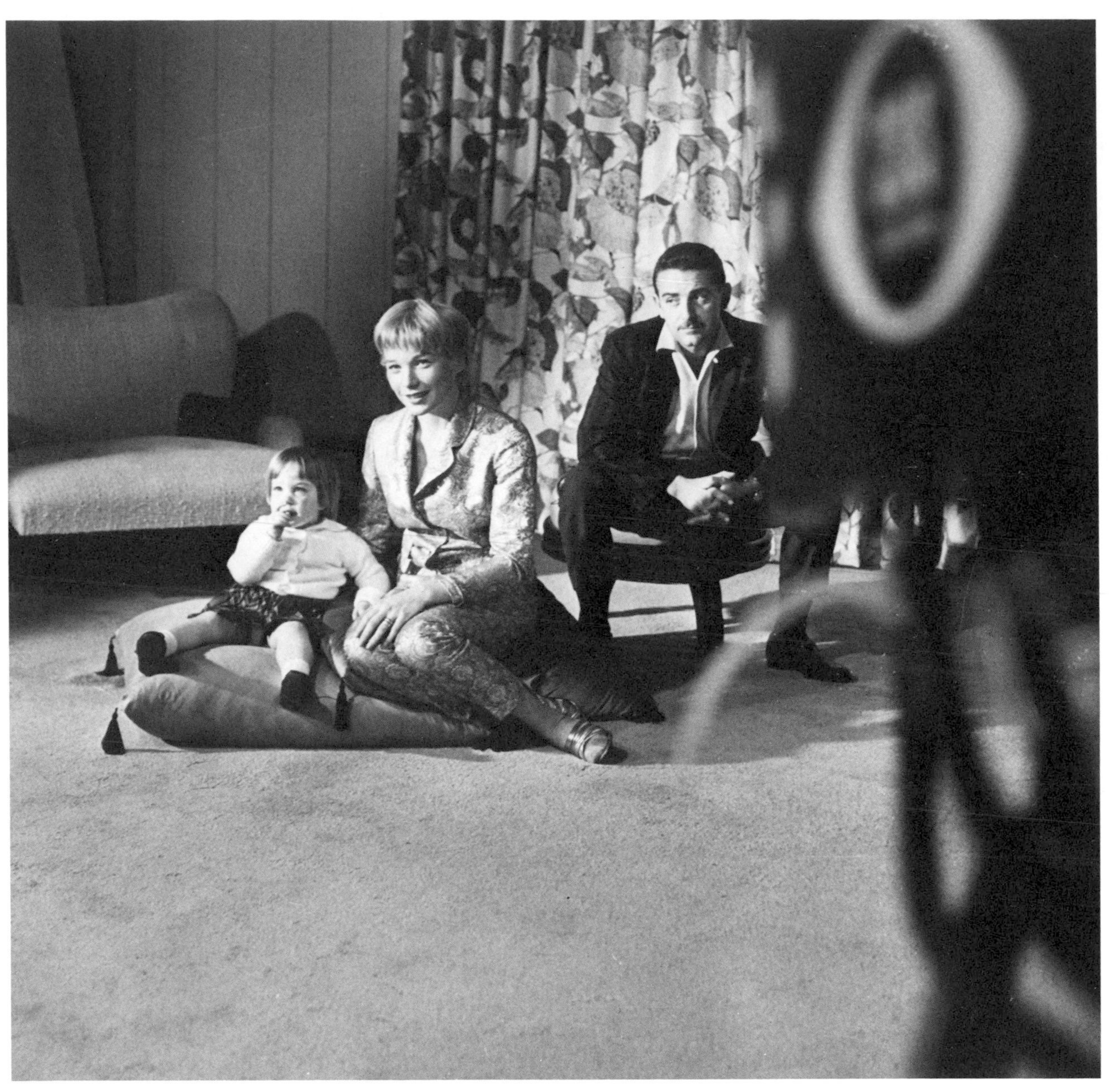

Left to right: Stephanie Sachiko Parker, Shirley MacLaine, and her husband, Steve Parker, as they appeared on CBS-TV's *Person to Person,* interviewed by Edward R. Murrow on March 6, 1959.

When Edward R. Murrow hosted his *Person to Person* series on CBS-TV Friday nights, it brought him new popularity. To his fame as a war correspondent, news commentator, and documentarian was added acclaim as an interviewer.

Person to Person extended Murrow's enormous prestige in the 1950s, and the great and the near great waited eagerly for a Murrow TV visit. It became clear that Murrow's show was an electronic Who's Who, and everyone wanted in.

Murrow interviewed the greats of his day—Bing Crosby, Marilyn Monroe, Liberace, the Duke and Duchess of Windsor, novelist James Jones, Marian Anderson. His interview with Shirley is one of his most entertaining.

Here is the complete transcript, March 6, 1959, 10:30 P.M. E.S.T.

MURROW: Good evening. I'm Ed Murrow. The name of the program is *Person to Person*. Tonight we'll be going to California for a visit with actress Shirley MacLaine and her family. We'll also be dropping in on Pulitzer Prize–winning cartoonist Rube Goldberg and his wife here in New York.

(Commercial)

MURROW: Shirley MacLaine is frequently described as the imp with the lawn-mower haircut. Along with her unusual hair style she has an unusual amount of style which she has demonstrated on Broadway and in Hollywood and on television. She is equally good as a singer, dancer, comedienne, and actress and is now a strong contender for the Academy Award as the best actress of the year for her performance in *Some Came Running*. Four years ago she was a seventy-five-dollar-a-week dancer in the chorus of a Broadway musical.

Shirley and her husband, Steve Parker, a television and motion-picture producer, have been married five years and have a two-year-old daughter. This is their home in Royal Oaks, California, overlooking San Fernando Valley, some five thousand miles from Japan, where they have a house and where Steve does much of his work. Evening, Shirley. Evening, Steve.

PARKER: Hi, Ed.

MACLAINE: Good evening, Ed.

MURROW: Good evening, Shirley. I don't want to start a family argument, but where would you rather be at this moment, California or Japan?

PARKER: We love both of them, Ed, but it's pretty hard to beat this California climate.

MURROW: Well, I imagine it takes a little juggling of your schedules so the two of you can be together. Shirley, how do you handle this problem?

MACLAINE: Well, at first it was a little difficult, Ed, but we worked it out, and for the last year and a half we both love to travel, so whenever I am off I take a quick jump for maybe three days to Japan or Hong Kong or wherever Steve is, and he comes back whenever he can. We are not separated much. We spend quite a bit of time together considering all the traveling we do.

MURROW: When are you going back, Steve?

PARKER: I'm going back tomorrow, Ed. I am in the middle of a lot of preproduction work for a film I am going to do this winter or early next year.

MURROW: You must feel pretty proud about that Academy Award nomination, don't you?

PARKER: I couldn't be prouder—wonderful!

MURROW: What about you, Shirley—a little bit nervous?

MACLAINE: Oh, I really am. It seems such a wonderful thing, Ed, to have such a good time working on a picture like I have been doing in *Some Came Running* with Frank Sinatra and also to think back . . . I have been a dancer all my life, since I was two and a half years old, and when I came to Hollywood in films I had never acted, I had only danced, so this is such a nice combination to be known only for acting. I love it.

MURROW: Perhaps you are better off if you never took any formal instruction in acting, would you think?

MACLAINE: Well, I think maybe I am. I don't think that Method kind of schooling would be good for me. It just doesn't seem to work. I more or less keep my eyes and ears open and watch things that go on around me and then, if I ever happen to use it in a scene, I do.

MURROW: Well, with Steve away from home so much you must find the evenings long and sometimes lonely, don't you?

MACLAINE: Well, they are, but most of our work . . . whenever he's gone . . . I've been awfully busy so that simultaneously the work occurred and by the time I got home from the studio every night, working from six to six-thirty, I was tired and only had time maybe to breathe and listen to music or watch television or something. Steve brought me some encyclopedias for Christmas, and I am up to the Y's now. I also love to read and study maps and find out where he is.

MURROW: Of course, I suppose fixing up the new house will keep you busy too, won't it?

MACLAINE: Oh, yes, Ed, that will be something. This, of course, is the first home we have ever owned, so it is quite an experience, and we don't have very much furniture. The furniture will be here Monday. There's none here now.

MURROW: Well, I am sure that Steve will find a few unusual things for you out in the Orient.

MACLAINE: Yes, he has. He has brought some back; a few of these pieces he brought back.

PARKER: You know, Ed, we used to have a real English-style home, and none of these Japanese things fit in it, but now that Shirley decided to move in here, I am real happy in this house. These things go really well with a modern home. Some of these things—this is a Korean chest I brought back from Korea.

MURROW: Yes.

PARKER: And a Kabuki dancer here—this is real interesting. Every Japanese home that has a daughter has one of these because it is a dream for a daughter really. It is a symbol of a husband and family and the entire life she would want. This is the husband and the wife and children, the retainers in the family, the warriors that guard the home. Every Japanese girl would like to have this type of home. The boys, of course, they have a carp, the pride of the house, a fish which is the symbol of courage, of course, because the carp is so strong, but we have a daughter, so we have to have this.

MURROW: Shirley, I understand you are quite a bargain hunter. Is this so?

MACLAINE: Oh, gracious me, I'm afraid I am. I have been that way all my life, and I love it. Sometimes I am penny wise and pound foolish. I went into a place, oh, I suppose five or so years ago. I will never forget. I saw a beautiful gown I wanted. I just wanted the dress; I didn't want the belt that went with it.

MURROW: Yes.

MACLAINE: And that was one of the first T-dresses.

MURROW: Shirley, where is your daughter tonight, asleep?

MACLAINE: Steppie?

MURROW: Yes.

MACLAINE: She is here. We worked out a schedule so that when we work we leave the house maybe at six in the morning and get home at six-thirty or seven at night and Stephanie or Steppie, as we call her, she goes to bed a little late too. Here she is now.

Hello, precious. Hello, sweetheart. Say hello to Mr. Murrow!

STEPPIE: Hello, Mr. Murrow.

MURROW: Hello, Steppie. How are you?

MACLAINE: Say, "I'm fine, Mr. Murrow."

STEPPIE: Fine, Mr. Murrow.

MURROW: How are you? No question who she looks like.

MACLAINE: No.

MURROW: Stephanie, I saw some photographs of you and your mother recently in *Life* magazine, making all sorts of funny faces. Shirley, do you think there is going to be another actress in the family?

MACLAINE: Well, I think maybe so.

PARKER: I think so.

MACLAINE: I think so. We go around most of the day making faces at each other.

Can you do that, sweetheart? You remember what we did on the picture?

MURROW: Wonderful.

MACLAINE: I think maybe.

MURROW: Yes.

MACLAINE: That's Daddy.

MURROW: That's Daddy. She'll recognize him. Shirley?

MACLAINE: Yes.

MURROW: You don't have to think back too far to your own childhood.

MACLAINE: There's not that much difference in our ages. That is why we get along so well. I can remember playing baseball with the fellows . . .

MURROW: What was your batting average?

MACLAINE: Batting average?

MURROW: Yes.

MACLAINE: .425—.425.

MURROW: You still play baseball?

MACLAINE: Oh, no, Ed. no. I gave that up when I was about fifteen. My batting average was good on baseball but not with the fellows, so I gave up baseball.

MURROW: Did you have that—

MACLAINE: Excuse me a moment. I think maybe I better put her to bed.

MURROW: Before you go, I wanted to know if you had that hairdo as a ballplayer.

MACLAINE: As a ballplayer?

MURROW: Yes.

MACLAINE: No, I got it when I was about, well, I suppose I was about, maybe, sixteen, in a Broadway show, and it was long; I used to have long red hair. Steve used to always tease me and whenever I did a pirouette, a turn on the stage, the audience's eyes were all going to me instead of the star, and I was just a chorus dancer. So the producer took me in between the first and second act one night, downstairs, and said, "Young lady, you cut your hair or otherwise you are out of this show."

So I dunked it in the sink and, of course, my hair was all wet and I didn't have too much time, and so my head is kind of pointed anyway, and it came up like this, and I got fired anyway!

MURROW: Steve, I meant to ask you this before. Why do you do so much of your work in Japan instead of here?

PARKER: Well, Ed, I have a firm belief that much of the future of the world lies in Asia and with the world getting so small with jet travel and modern age and quicker travel upon us, it will only be a matter of one or two more years before going to Tokyo is as simple as traveling from Los Angeles to New York. It's going to take a lot of understanding between peoples, and I don't think there is any better medium than the visual medium of motion pictures and television to teach people to understand each other, and I would like to be a part of that when it happens.

MURROW: What's the reaction in the Orient to the movies Hollywood is turning out these days, Steve?

PARKER: Well, in the Orient, they are very influenced; the people are very influenced by American films, and whatever they see they take for granted as being a part of American life, and I think here that more time should be given to the content of films that we export abroad, because it does affect these people tremendously, and we should show them the honest side of it instead of the crime and etc. It has a tremendous effect on them.

MURROW: Shirley, very few people in show business have come along as fast and successfully as you have. What would you say was the big turning point?

MACLAINE: Well, frankly, I did work awfully hard from the time I was two. The turning point came, a break, when I was in a show called *Pajama Game*.

MURROW: Yes.

MACLAINE: I was a chorus dancer and had a few lines to sing because I sang loud, that was all, and the star of the show, the hit of the show, was a woman named Carol Haney.

MURROW: Yes.

MACLAINE: A wonderful girl . . . and she broke her ankle the very night of the show, and I, as her understudy, went on, and then I was signed by Mr. Hitchcock and Mr. Wallis, and I came to Hollywood and the same thing happened in television. Betty Grable broke her leg before a big show, and naturally they called me and so I did it. I suppose that someday something will happen to me and maybe my understudy will go on, and I hope she is as lucky as I was.

PARKER: We have someone waiting for you right now.

MACLAINE: That's so.

MURROW: Shirley, you are frequently described in print as one of Hollywood's more rugged individualists. Are you?

MACLAINE: Well, Ed, I really like to be myself. I have no time to do anything else. I enjoy it, and I hope I don't hurt anyone's feelings by sometimes being frank and too honest and speaking my mind, but that is the way I am. If that means I am a rugged individualist, then I am.

MURROW: And your marriage seems to have worked out very well too, despite the long separation because of Steve's work in Japan.

MACLAINE: It has, Ed. It certainly has. We feel and I feel very strongly that what Steve is doing is tremendously important. It is vital to not only the film industry or the television industry like the Japanese show that we did, but it is important to the people on both sides of the world because he is really acting as more or less an intermediary between the two cultures. He understands them and portrays them authentically, and I think they appreciate that and have more of a co-production feeling—if we could all get together. This is something both Steve and I feel is bigger than us.

MURROW: Well, much luck to the both of you.

MACLAINE: Thank you.

MURROW: Thank you, Shirley, for letting us come. Good night, Steve.

PARKER: Good night.

MACLAINE: Good night.

MURROW: Have a very safe trip back to Japan, and Shirley, good luck on the Academy Award.

MACLAINE: Thank you very much.

Shirley MacLaine on Stage

Shirley MacLaine, second from left, a struggling unknown dancer in the chorus of *Me and Juliet,* rehearsing in costume, May 1953.

Shirley, second from right, listens silently to instructions on the set of *Me and Juliet* during this dance rehearsal.

In the summer of 1950, Shirley, all of sixteen years old, convinced her parents to let her take a crack at studying and perhaps working in New York City, during her hiatus from high school.

Shortly after arrival, she found a job working in the chorus line of the City Center's revival of *Oklahoma!* At the finish of the run, the entire production was invited to play at the Berlin Arts Festival. Shirley's decision was to return to Arlington and finish high school, which she did.

Two years and one high school diploma later, Shirley was back in New York looking for work in show business. After several jobs dancing in trade shows, mostly outside New York, she finally landed a job in the chorus line of Rodgers and Hammerstein's musical comedy *Me and Juliet,* after three stubborn attempts.

Me and Juliet opened May 28, 1953, at the Majestic Theatre, starring Isabel Bigley, Bill Hayes, Joan McCracken, and Ray Walston. Though decidedly not one of Rodgers and Hammerstein's best efforts, it ran a breezy 358 performances.

Said the respected theater critic of the *New York Times,* Brooks Atkinson: "When Mr. Rodgers and Mr. Hammerstein make up their minds what they are writing about, *Me and Juliet* may turn out to be an enjoyable show. . . . It has just about everything except an intelligible story." As for the cast, he added: *"Me and Juliet* is cast with nothing but thoroughbreds."

It was during the run of this show that Shirley cut her hair to its now famous "eggbeater style." Richard Rodgers saw Shirley doing leaps and turns during the rehearsal of the chorus and watched as her then very long auburn hair smacked her in the face with each completed turn. He quickly and sternly advised her to cut it. Shirley went backstage, grabbed a pair of scissors, and speedily reappeared with the haircut that is now her trademark.

The Pajama Game, a musical based on a novel by Richard Bissell, *7½ Cents,* about life, love, and labor relations in an Iowa pajama factory, next attracted Shirley. Routinely, she went to audition and was selected. Director George Abbott later told Shirley he hired her because, Shirley happily recalls, "whenever I opened my mouth on stage they could hear every breath in the peanut gallery."

Out of town the word was that the show would definitely be a smash in New York and that the show would give Broadway a new star, dancer-comedienne Carol Hancy. On May 9, 1954, the show previewed at the St. James. By opening night, May 13, Carol Haney was the sensation of Broadway and *Pajama Game* was a solid hit assured of a long money-making run on Broadway.

Contrarily, Shirley was gloomy at the prospect of a long run, knowing she'd be bored to death just bumping along in the chorus night after night. The night before the opening Shirley was made understudy to Carol Haney. The show opened with Shirley never having had an understudy rehearsal. Producer Hal Prince remarked to Shirley, "It doesn't matter. Carol is the one person who would go on with a broken neck."

Brooks Atkinson of the *New York Times* said in his review: "The last new musical of the season is the best. It is *The Pajama Game,* which opened at the St. James last evening with all the uproar of a George Abbott show." Of Carol Haney, Atkinson said: "She is a comic dancer of extraordinary versatility. Shaggy haired and gamin like, she suits the mode. . . . Both as dancer and actress Miss Haney is superb."

Four nights into the show, Carol Haney broke her ankle, and Shirley MacLaine became

Shirley, second row, seventh from left with big smile, during curtain call in *Me and Juliet,* 1953. This photo is from the star of the show, Bill Hayes, first row, tenth from left.

the second overnight sensation to come out of that show. Fatefully, the evening she went on for Haney, Shirley had arrived at the theater with her termination notice in hand.

She was rushed onstage by producer Hal Prince with the words: "Carol Haney broke her ankle this afternoon, and you're on right now!" Somehow, she made it through the show, and when the final curtain rang down, Shirley recalled in her autobiography, *Don't Fall Off the Mountain:* "The audience stood. They cheered—and threw kisses. I felt as though a giant caress had enveloped me. The cast backed off, formed a circle around me, and applauded."

A new star was born.

Shirley's next venture into legitimate theater came soon after the birth of Sachie in 1956. Her pregnancy prevented her from accepting film offers, so when a co-starring role in the West Coast touring version of Terence Rattigan's *The Sleeping Prince* opened up, Shirley eagerly grabbed it.

She co-starred with Francis Lederer and Hermione Gingold in this comedy tale of an American chorus girl courted by a suave European prince in Edwardian London. (When the story was made into a film in 1957, it was called *The Prince and the Showgirl* and starred Laurence Olivier and Marilyn Monroe.)

The play debuted at the Huntington Hartford Theatre in Los Angeles on November 28, 1956, to excellent critical notices, but fared

Shirley shakes hands with adoring fans at the close of her record-breaking run at New York City's Palace Theatre in 1976.

poorly at the box office. When the tour finished in San Francisco thirteen weeks later, however, it had made enough money to make up for its initial slow start.

Said *Variety:* "The show is a triumph for Miss MacLaine, and stamps her as a bright comedy talent combining perception and variation to create a character that lives and sparkles."

Shirley did no legitimate theater anywhere after that and did not return to Broadway until twenty years later. On February 2, 1976, Shirley made her live stage debut outside the United States when she appeared at the famous London Palladium, where she broke box-office records during a limited two-week engagement and was adored by fans and critics alike.

"From the moment she propelled herself onto the stage, Miss MacLaine proclaimed her right to be mentioned in the same breath as Judy Garland, Mary Martin, Ethel Merman, Liza Minnelli and other queens of American show business," said the *Evening Standard* of London.

"This offbeat, scatty creature with a sheepdog haircut and irrepressible high spirits hit us between the eyes from the start," noted the *London Evening News.*

That marked the beginning of a worldwide tour that took her to Paris, Madrid, Monte Carlo, and Rio de Janeiro, as well as cities throughout the United States, climaxing in New York City at the Palace Theatre.

On April 19, 1976, Shirley MacLaine opened at the Palace for a two-week engagement that set a new all-time box-office record in the then sixty-three-year history of that theater. The house was standing room only, and at the end of the engagement the show had grossed more than $329,000.

Wrote the *New York Daily News:* "The pixyish quality that lifted that polished gamin, Shirley MacLaine, out of the chorus of *The Pajama Game* in 1954, and made her a movie star in no time at all is the attractive, unifying element of the brassy, Las Vegas–type stage show she brought to the Palace last evening. For close to an hour and a half (there is no intermission), the trim and engaging Miss MacLaine sings, dances, catches her breath and chats, with the assistance of five young dancers and a 27-piece band spread out across the rear of the stage. And though everything is neatly packaged and tied with a bow for a mass audience, the star's engaging personality keeps inserting little grace notes into a show that is all too typically designed to kill."

The *New York Times* said, "It is 20 years since Shirley MacLaine took her long legs and wonderful smile off to Hollywood. Back on Broadway for a two-week run, she has brought with her all the aging of those twenty years and hardly any of their growth. . . . Miss MacLaine is only a fair singer and she is even less of a belter. . . . Her dancing is considerably more persuasive. . . . There are moments, usually quiet moments and throwaway lines when Miss MacLaine's face recaptures its old magic. Small rebellious bursts of greed, lust, outrage, joy—always contained. The beauty of her smile used to be its moorings. . . . She has personality, but she withholds it."

However the critics felt, the audiences showed up in droves and had nothing but sheer admiration for Shirley's performance. Shirley later reflected to the *New York Times:* "I hadn't been on stage in twenty years, but dancing is like yoga, or driving a car. Once you learn, you never forget it." Yet whenever she goes back onstage, she says, "I feel terror, sheer, pure, unadulterated terror from top to bottom. These people who get a laugh and then relax—that's not me. Being a dancer, I'm a masochist, and so I must love fright. Frank, Liza, and Sammy say that I'll never get over it and that I shouldn't. They say that when they forget to be afraid, then they're not as good." And finally, "You're up there all alone—you're not playing a role, you're playing yourself. And if it bombs, there's nobody else to blame."

Shirley MacLaine in Nightclubs

Shirley, at Riviera, sings the poignant "Remember Me?" a song that chronicles her career from the chorus line to stardom.

Shirley and "Shirley's Gypsies" performing the exquisite "Steam Heat" number from *Pajama Game* at the Riviera Hotel in Las Vegas.

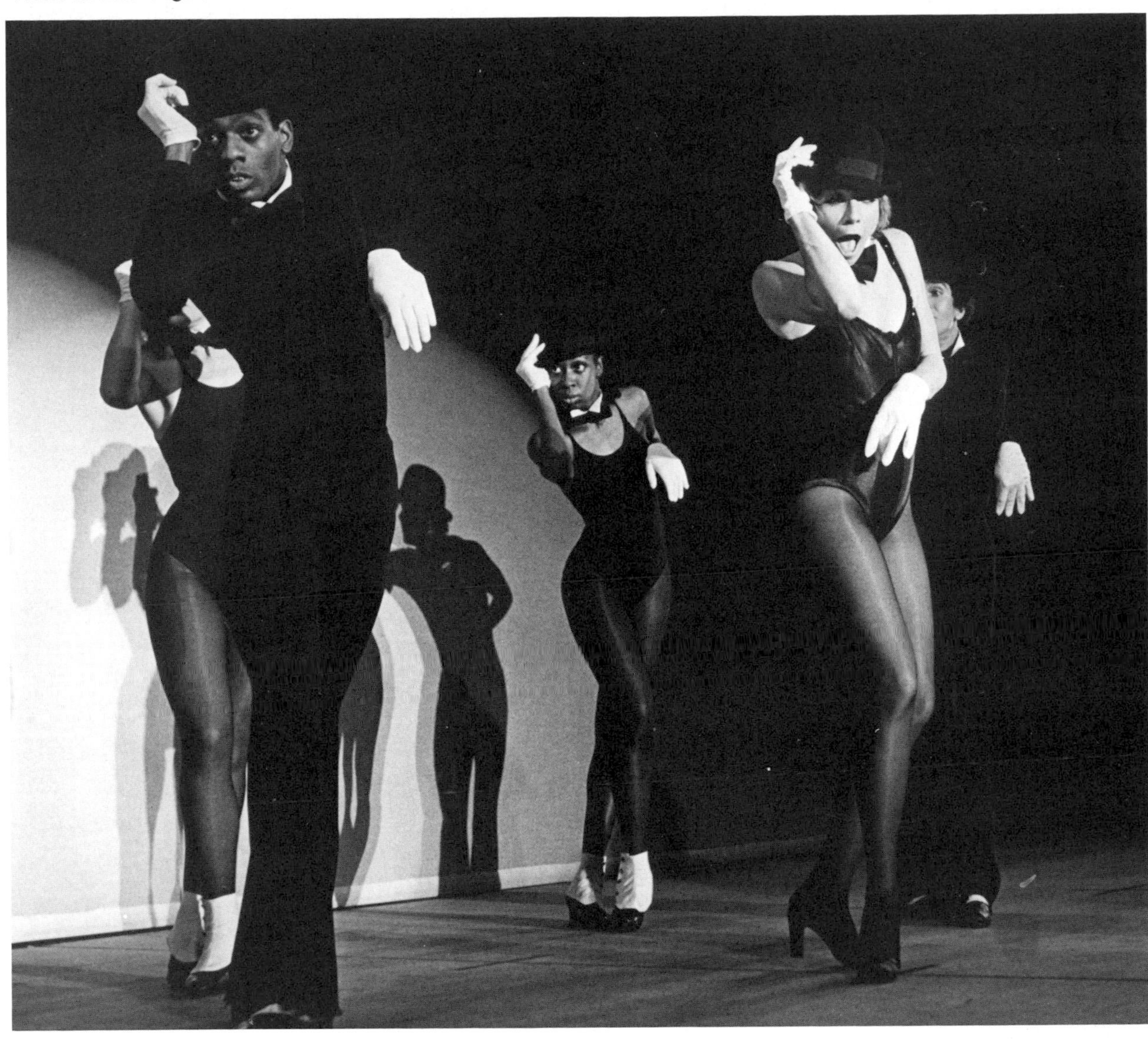

Shirley MacLaine went directly from hometown dance lessons to New York and chorus-girl jobs in Broadway musicals. Then when she became a movie star, she periodically returned to the stage for concerts, did the rounds of TV talk shows, TV specials, and even one TV series, then filled in with occasional nightclub dates.

It was inevitable that she'd work the Las Vegas hotels—now using more variety-stage acts than any other place in the world. She premiered her revue at the MGM Grand in 1974, then headlined at Caesars Palace. She then appeared at the Golden Nugget in Sparks, Nevada, and during the past few years, she has been playing the Riviera Hotel.

Backed by four "dance gypsies," she's amazingly agile for her age, doing high kicks and strenuous modern dances. Interlaced are songs about her life and career, in which she drops comments like, "I knew Sinatra when he was a Democrat" and "What's the difference between Panama Canal and Anita Bryant? Well, the canal is a busy ditch. . . ."

In her café act, she often comments about her movie career. She recalls, for instance, that Billy Wilder, who directed her in *Irma la Douce,* told her, "It's very important that the actress playing a lady of the evening try not to seem to be enjoying her work" and that when Shirley played a hooker "you look like a secretary typing a letter."

Shirley insists she always researched her

Shirley delights the audience at the Riviera, saying, "Sure I'd play a hooker again, if she got to be Secretary of State."

roles as a hooker, and "I got to like the research better than the acting!"

Her shows in Las Vegas have always been and continue to be sellouts and standing room only.

Shirley has returned to Las Vegas and the Riviera, and with each engagement, her act gets stronger and smoother. On October 13, 1978, the *Las Vegas Sun* reviewed her show:

"Shirley MacLaine's friends will have to hurry to make reservations for the Versailles Theatre in the Riviera Hotel if they want to 'see her now.' Shirley and Fred Travalena, who produces one devastating impression after another, packed the Strip room opening night. . . . She remains onstage almost throughout the entire hour, singing, dancing, laughing and even crying when she describes her scene with Frank Sinatra in *Some Came Running* as she tells him, 'I'm a Person Too.' The high point of the dance routine is the characterization of four styles of dance—as conceived by choreographers Bob Fosse,

Backed by her "gypsies," Shirley cuts loose here, showing club-goers what many call "the most beautiful legs in Hollywood."

At Caesars Palace, Shirley and her dancers knock out a show-stopping rendition of "If My Friends Could See Me Now."

"What America needs now is a little fun. And so I decided to do something about it," Shirley told audiences at the Riviera Hotel.

Shirley told fans at Caesars Palace, "I went back to the gym, ran five miles a day, quit smoking, and got an act together."

Michael Kidd, Alan Johnson and the black influence. . . . Shirley complains about pace, sits on the stage, 'puffed out,' and then goes right back into another strenuous routine that would tax a younger person. 'Imagine me with a 22-year-old daughter!' she says, as she executes one high kick after another. The entire production runs with clockwork precision."

Variety said: "The Shirley MacLaine opus with Fred Travalena has all of the peak entertainment elements within a 90 minute span. MacLaine's rigorous song-and-dance act is something special as she guides her four gypsies—Claire Culhane, Larry Vickers, Jamilah Hunter and Vincent Patterson—through some impressive choreos and stands alone in both poignant and funny remembrances from past films."

The *Las Vegas Mirror* echoed: "If you haven't seen Shirley MacLaine perform live, catch her act at the Riviera. The lady is a true professional, at ease with herself and the audience, controlling the stage at all times, even when kidding with first-night talkers in the audience. How this mother of a 22-year-old daughter keeps up the pace with two shows nightly is beyond me."

In 1976, Shirley won the Female Musical Star of the Year honors in the annual Las Vegas Entertainment Awards ceremony. In 1977, she was finalist in the same category.

Shirley has also taken her nightclub act to Australia and met with magnificent reviews and audience response.

A Shirley MacLaine

Portrait Gallery

1064-(69-3)

SOMEBODY UP THERE LIKES ME
ROCKY GRAZIANO
WRITTEN WITH ROLAND BARBER